Sing God A Simple Song

To Marjorie,

With happy memories

of our weekend together in

Atlanta!   Peace & love

Betty Buckingham

Sing God A Simple Song

Exploring music in worship for the eighties

Betty Pulkingham

An Albatross Book
Marshall Pickering

Marshall Morgan and Scott
Marshall Pickering
3 Beggarwood Lane, Basingstoke, Hants RG23 7LP, UK

First published in 1986 by Marshall Morgan and Scott Publications Ltd
Part of the Marshall Pickering Holdings Group
A subsidiary of the Zondervan Corporation
Co-publishers: Albatross Books, PO Box 320, Sutherland, NSW 2232,
Australia

British Library Cataloguing in Publication Data

Pulkingham, Betty
    Sing God a simple song: exploring music in worship
    for the eighties
    1. Music in churches   2. Church music
    History and criticism
    I. Title
    264'.2   BV290

ISBN 0–551–01317–6

Phototypeset in Linotron Palatino by
Input Typesetting Ltd, London
Printed in Great Britain by Hazell Watson & Viney Ltd,
member of the BPCC Group, Aylesbury, Bucks

For all the members of the
Society of the Community of Celebration

Acknowledgements

I would like to thank a host of friends and companions in the Way, whose lives and ministries have affected my own and served as a stimulus for the writing of this book. Here I can mention only a few. First, I would like to thank my husband Graham, whose love of God and of God's people continues to be a constant source of inspiration and challenge to me in my own spiritual journey. I am grateful to Roland Walls, from the Community of the Transfiguration, for allowing us from the Community of Celebration to sit at his feet and learn about the theology of worship. I am grateful to the Fisherfolk International Team, with whom I have lived and travelled for the past three years, for their willingness to experiment with many of my fledgling ideas; to Arabella Kornahrens, for editorial work on the manuscript; to Martha Barker, for her contributions to Chapter 2; to Mark Durie, whose ideas were a springboard for Chapter 5; to Kevin Hackett, for his uncanny ability to find any bit of research material that I required; to Steven Plummer, for his tireless work as typist; to Cathleen Morris for proof-reading. Finally, I would like to thank all those around the world whose songs and faces and questions and letters have given me the inspiration and desire to write this book.

Betty Pulkingham

Contents

Foreword
  1: The Song . . . a personal journey
  2: An Hour on Sunday?
     . . . understanding worship
  3: Building Worship Together
     . . . understanding liturgy
  4: When We Gather . . . more about liturgy
  5: Simple is Beautiful . . . the church's folk music
  6: Pulling Out All the Stops
     . . . the musicians' pastoral role
  7: Follow the Leader . . . folk leadership in worship
  8: Choirs Ancient and Modern . . . which is yours?
  9: Prelude to Praise . . . what is a good rehearsal?
 10: New Wineskins . . . the church – a crucible for
     creativity

Foreword

Music has always been a force for bringing people together. Because of this its value as a worship tool for both tiny church and massive cathedral is priceless.

There is a very thin dividing line between fine art (e.g. the singing of choral evensong in an Anglican cathedral) and folk art which, *Sing God a Simple Song* argues, is of greater benefit to participation in community worship. With experience culled from years of pioneering achievement at the Church of the Redeemer in Houston, Texas, with the Fisherfolk ministries, and with the Community of Celebration, Isle of Cumbrae, Scotland, Betty Pulkingham stresses the merits of the folk arts in single acts of corporate praise.

For too many years, music in our churches has often been dull and meaningless. The author suggests new ways in which all can become involved in the 'peoples' work' – liturgy. In some cases, liturgical bounds need to be widened, in some cases torn down so that spontaneity can work hand in hand with well tried order.

Church music has been one of the few, perhaps the only, unifying feature in inter-denominational ecclesiastical history. We must by all means rediscover its unifying and evangelistic potential in the church today.

George McPhee
Paisley Abbey,
June 1985

1: The Song . . . a personal journey

> *There is no bird on the wing,*
> *There is no star in the sky,*
> *There is nothing beneath the sun,*
> *But proclaims His goodness.*
> *Jesu! Jesu! Jesu!*
> *Jesu! meet it were to praise Him.*[1]

There is a dance to be danced. There is a song to be sung. And that's all there is to it. God **has** come to us, permeating this earth/creation with divine presence. Should we neglect to respond to God's giving to us, the very stones would burst into song! For response there must be. There is a praising music in the universe and we can tune our ears to hear it if we so desire.

St. Francis heard it. Recovering from an illness which had affected his eyes and kept him confined in a darkened cell for fifty days, he was sunning himself in the garden one morning and waiting for St. Clare, when he suddenly heard the praising music of the universe. Raising his hands in joyful response he sang:

> *Oh most high, almighty, good Lord God,*
> *to thee belong praise, glory, honour and all blessing!*
>
> *Praised be my Lord God with all His creatures;*
> *and specially our brother the sun,*
> *who brings us the day and who brings us the light;*
> *fair is he, and shining with very great*
> *splendour. . .*

11

Praised be my Lord for our sister the moon,
  and for the stars
The which He has set clear and lovely in heaven. . .[2]

The lapping waters praise God; God hears the gentle sound and says, 'It is good.' The birds praise God in their singing, the flowers in their blooming. That seems simple. But what about us? How shall *we* praise God? If that were only one question I dare say we should soon have our answers. But other questions seem to crowd in, destroying the primeval simplicity.

Why, after all, should we praise God when the world God made is in such a mess and fraught with injustice and suffering on every side? *When* shall we praise God? Because, after all, there is work to be done, crying needs to be met, and that is important. The *whys* and *whens* soon crowd out the still small voice of *how*. If the *whens* have their way, then life divides into times of praising God and times of not praising God; times when we get on with the ordinary business of life. If the *whys* have their way we may never get around to praising God at all! For we will not have accepted St. Francis' first premise, that praise belongs to God, is God's by right and that God deserves our praise.

It is the premise of this small book that God **is worthy** to be praised at all times and in all places; and so to move past the *whens* and *whys* to the question of how we go about it. I am writing to all who have a particular concern for the corporate worship of the church today. How can we deepen our own personal praise experience, and how can we impart a vision to the gathered church, Christ's body?

First of all, perhaps we can learn from St. Francis' perspective, for he saw himself as one of many praising creatures. He called the sun 'brother', the moon 'sister'; as a member of creation's family of praise, Francis did not think of himself more highly than he did of the rest of God's creation. How would he have reacted, I wonder, to the modern liturgist's abbreviated use of the *Benedicite, omnia opera* – the one which skirts past the entire cosmic order, the earth and all its creatures, and begins, 'O ye people of God, bless ye the Lord; O ye priests of the Lord, bless ye the Lord'? It seems difficult for us, living in a world whose temper is humanism and whose trust tends towards the work of human hands, to take our rightful place as one of many members in the community of creation's praise.

The story is told of a medieval divine, St. Benno, who used to roam the pasturelands beyond the monastery, singing praises to the Lord as a part of his daily devotions. One day his cantillation was disturbed by a loudly croaking frog who, like St Benno, had positioned himself in the meadow. The saint became irritated at the persistent sounds of the frog, and finally in desperation said to the frog, 'Shut up!' Later that same day, the story continues, when he was back within the monastery walls, the saint's conscience was smitten by the memory of this frog. Retracing his steps to the meadow, he searched diligently to find the wee creature, whose croaking praise (the Holy Spirit had shown him) was not to be despised. He asked the frog's forgiveness.

Without drawing any pointed parallels between the croaking frog and the person beside us in the church pew, it is safe to say that most of us do have aesthetic standards of some sort, and find ourselves irritated by – what: a crying baby; the rhythmic roof-leak that pings into a metal pail; the post-menopausal vibrato behind us? We too, like St Benno and St Francis, have need of identifying ourselves with creation, remembering that it is God who designed this motley chorus!

But what, after all, is unique about *our* praises, as

distinct from stones or flowers or singing birds? Is it not this: that we are free to respond, and it is our free response that makes God happy? 'How can the likes of me make God happy?' one may ask. I believe that one of the keys to fervent praise is knowing that we *can* make God happy by our offering of a sacrifice of praise and thanksgiving.

Twice in my lifetime the Holy Spirit has spoken to me unmistakably about praise. The first time I was attending a service in a dimly lit church, one-third full of people whose participation could be described only generously as 'half-hearted'. I cannot say what affected me most: the depressing effect of the poorly lit church building, or the equally depressing thought that no one seemed to have noticed the difficulty people were having in reading from their hymnals and prayer books. I only know that my spirit was deeply troubled. In the midst of my unrest and against the dismal backdrop of the situation, God's desire for a praising people suddenly stood out. The words 'Let every creature that hath breath praise the Lord' burst upon my consciousness.

Let every creature that hath breath praise the Lord. God created in order to bring about praise; creation reaches its own fulfilment in praise. Our bodies are designed to *breathe* praise, to experience the adoration of God moment by moment throughout our limited days. Small wonder, I thought, that the psalms are full of commands to 'sing to the Lord'. We have received breath in order to sing God's praises! Why *not* sing to God? Why *not* open our hearts in praise to the King of kings and Lord of lords? Suddenly the desire for this people, presently assembled with me at a particular time and place, to be released into God's high praises, was so powerfully present that I knew God would perform a miracle in their midst! I knew in that moment that it was God's will, God's ardent desire, God's intention to release these very people into praise. And I knew that I would work with God to bring it about.

The Psalmist tells us that God abides in the praises of his people, that God is at home there, that God likes it there. It is not sufficient for us, it would seem, to know that God is *worthy* of praise; we must somehow know that it matters to him, that it pleases our Father in heaven or us to praise him. In relating to God as Father, Jesus has shown us the way to a personal relationship, a new dimension of knowing the same God who meted out the heavens in a span. Jesus Christ has shown us what it means to offer a sacrifice of praise and thanksgiving.

The second revelation about praise came to me as I was reading the Old Testament in my bedroom one day. The setting is this: the priests brought the ark of the Lord's covenant to its place in the inner sanctuary of the temple; then they withdrew from the holy place. All the priests, regardless of their divisions, consecrated themselves. All the Levites, who were musicians, stood on the east side of the altar, dressed in fine linen and playing cymbals, harps and lyres, accompanied by one hundred and twenty priests sounding trumpets.

> *The trumpeters and singers joined in unison, AS WITH ONE VOICE, to give praise and thanks to the Lord. Accompanied by trumpets, cymbals, and other instruments, they raised their voices in praise to the Lord and sang, 'He is good; his love endures for ever.'*
> *Then the temple of the Lord was filled with a cloud,* and the priests could not perform their service because of the cloud, for the glory of the Lord filled the temple of God* (2 Chronicles 5:13–14).

At this point in time I can only remember that the impact of this passage was so strong that I found myself, quite literally, prostrate on the bedroom floor. It was as if the Lord had pulled aside the curtains of time and space and had granted me a first-hand vision of this 'Shekinah' glory. The strength of the vision lay not in the numbers of instruments or singers or trumpeting priests; the strength lay in the UNITY of their offering. They joined 'AS WITH ONE VOICE' to give praise and thanks to God. This powerful unity was beyond comprehension, yet it was a fact. When they were before God AS ONE, God's glory filled the temple.

To attempt to translate such beauty, such unity, such a happening, into the ordinariness of twentieth century church life – who could dare to try? And yet, wonder of wonders, audacity of audacities, God was clearly saying to me, 'This vision is for my people here – today! If they will continually come before me in praise of my glory, if they will submit their lives to the costly discipline of unity, my glory will fill their assembly, and I will dwell in their midst with power.'

At the time the vision came to me I was a busy homemaker and mother of five children. We lived in the city and I knew only too well the difficulties of getting a household of eight to ten people together just for an evening meal; never mind the praying and singing! (And the thought of a hundred and twenty well-tuned trumpets caused the mind to boggle!) In my experience, even the simplest type of unity, i.e., doing the same thing at the same time, seemed incredibly difficult in our pluralistic, urban society. Yet there it was: costly unity, powerful, praise-filled worship of God, in a dynamic equation strong enough to knock me off my feet.

The two revelations just recounted have shaped and coloured my own relationship to the Godhead. In the first instance, knowing God's deep desire for a praising people kindled in me a desire to respond. I wanted more than anything else to *live* in God's

16

praises! And secondly, I saw the corporate dimension of such a life as the place where God would make his home, would dwell in power. If his people would come together as one to offer him praise, if they would make this offering the fulcrum of their lives, he would be present to them in such a consistent and powerful way that one could truly say God's glory had *filled that house*.

From the time I was a young girl there were two things which gave me equal delight. One was making music with people. When first learning part-singing I would come home from school, teach my mother the melody and my aunt the alto part; then I would sing the part in the middle and direct! The other recollection (when I was younger still) was of family gatherings where I liked to play 'shoe store', removing everyone's shoes and 'trying on' different ones. I can still recall the utter delight of viewing a room full of bare feet!

Now the question is this: was God somehow preparing me for a vision yet to come? In my flights of fantasy I like to think so. Preparing for a place where we would all remove from our feet our shoes of anxiety, of fretful caring for life's details, because we would know we were standing on holy ground. And this holy ground – where is it? Is it not the place God chooses to dwell in and manifest himself to us? This is the place where each of us will learn to sing a particular part in creation's praising chorus. We will come *as one* before the Lord, the Creator of heaven and earth, the Redeemer and Holy One of Israel; the Spirit and sanctifier of the faithful; the one triune God. To him be praise, as is meet, forever and forever. Amen.

2: An Hour on Sunday? . . .
understanding worship

See all the crazy dances that I can do
on top of hazy mountains, singing to you
a song for celebrating every day new.
    Isn't it good, Father?
    Isn't it good?

I love to feel the morning smiling on me,
warming the tops of the mountain and trees,
Loveliest sight for somebody to see!
    Isn't it good, Father?
    Isn't it good?![1]

What is worship? The response of the created being to the Creator of all things? The warm awareness of a sustaining presence in a world of violence? It is this and more. Worship is a song for celebrating the goodness of God, a basic awareness of who God is and who we are! Worship is wonder, the wonder of the created being beholding the beauty of creation, contemplating the mystery of the Trinity, trying to fathom the unfathomable love of God.

Worship is . . . an hour on Sunday? So many would say. Frequently we fall into thinking of worship as a specific event happening at a specific place. 'We're going to morning worship', we say, and by that we mean a certain place and a predictable time (and heaven forbid that we extend the boundaries!) What we do while there is to 'worship', by which we generally mean some combination of singing, praying, preaching, listening. I would like

18

to explore with you a concept of worship which goes beyond the specific to the general, beyond the categorical to the whole.

Worship involves all of life

Worship, far from being a specific event or a category of life, concerns all of life. It has to do with everything we do, and everything we don't do. It has to do with how we feel, the things we think about, the problems we have, the things with which we struggle. It is not, in the final analysis, something we do at all. It is rather a generic term to describe a relationship between us as people and whatever he, she or it is to whom we ascribe worth.* C. S. Lewis had it right when he said,

> *'The world rings with praise: lovers praising their mistresses, readers their favourite poet, walkers praising the countryside, players praising their favourite game; praise of weather, wine, dishes, actors, motors, horses, colleges, countries, historical personages, children, flowers, mountains, rare stamps, rare beetles, or even sometimes politicians or scholars . . . just as men spontaneously praise whatever they value, so they spontaneously urge us to join them in praising it.*
> *'Isn't she lovely!' 'Wasn't it glorious!' 'Don't you think that magnificent?' The Psalmists, in telling everyone to praise God, are doing what men do when they speak of what they care about.'[2]*

As surely as the sun rises and sets, we human beings care about and praise something or someone. We are in our most essential being worshippers. When we were created in God's image we were given an ability for relationship, the same sort of relation-

* worship [Anglo-Saxon *weorthscipe*], to ascribe worth.

ship as expressed in the Trinity. In saying, 'Let us create', God was revealing the essence of the divine identity. God is, in very being, a community of persons. 'Let us create someone', said God, 'who can enter into relationship. Like us!' God wanted created beings to enjoy the same fellowship that the Godhead: Father, Son and Spirit, knew among themselves. This capacity for relationship is our birthright as human beings.

With infinite wisdom God set limits for us as creatures. God told Adam and Eve not to eat the fruit of a particular tree – the tree of the knowledge of good and evil. Clearly, we are not independent creatures, although we have been given spiritual lordship and power.

> Then God said, 'Let us make man in our image, in our likeness, and let them rule over the fish of the sea and the birds of the air, over the livestock, over all the earth, and over all the creatures that move along the ground.' So God created man in His own image, in the image of God He created him; male and female He created them. God blessed them and said to them, 'Be fruitful and increase in number; fill the earth and subdue it (Gen. 1:26–8).

This lordship entrusted to humankind by God is not in any way independent. Indeed, we are very dependent on God.

> When you open your hand, they are satisfied with good things. When you hide your face, they are terrified; when you take away their breath, they die and return to the dust. When you send your spirit, they are created, and you renew the face of the earth (Ps. 104:28b–30).

When we human beings try to assert our independence, the fruit of that assertion is suffering, alienation from another and from God. God waits for us at the crossroads where we followed the 'Independence' signpost. He does not abandon us, but he does give us the freedom to explore this route of alienation, separation and grief. He allows us to choose freely how we will live in this world.

We live in a secular age

How do we live in this contemporary world? This is the age variously described as the 'age of technology', the 'age of expertise'. There was a time when theologians and the leaders of governments exercised great authority. But perceptive thinkers today are challenging us to look beneath the surface of modern society and recognize the immense power of technology to control our leaders.

> *A spectre is stalking in our midst whom only a few see with clarity. It is not the old ghost of communism or fascism. It is a new spectre: a completely mechanized society, devoted to maximal material output and consumption, directed by computers; and in this social process man himself is being transformed into a part of the total machine; well fed and entertained, yet passive, unalive and with little feeling.[3]*

Behind every government official is a string of computer printouts that pretty well steers the ship of state. A frightening thought? Perhaps. But let us consider the effect of the technological age on the individual. As an expert in an age of specialization, each one of us seems to be learning more and more about less and less! There is a curious kind of isolation that characterizes the expert. As he or she becomes increasingly skilled in one particular area of expertise, there may be less opportunity and a diminishing ability to communicate broadly. Rarified

21

bits of knowledge seem to set one apart from one's neighbours. Language, the communication tool *par excellence* down through the ages, becomes jargon-esque, and only the inner circle will readily recognize such language code as 'AMR', or 'AGO', or 'WCC'.* An American bishop, discerning the hazards of professional cliques, once said, 'The clergy are just like fertilizer. When you spread them through the kingdom, they cause things to grow and there's a fruitful harvest. Yep, just like fertilizer. When you put them in a heap together, THEY STINK!'

Perhaps there is, when all is said and done, a putrefaction process that is likely to happen to the 'expert' in our age; in ways more or less subtle, the expert can be separated from the human community which his or her profession is designed to serve. Certainly there was a time in history when trained musicians knew a lot about theology, and theologians about music. In such an age one would be less likely to hear of events such as the one reported in a British newspaper recently where an English vicar and his parish organist came to blows in the organ loft over the choice of an evening hymn! While this may seem extreme, I would contend that there are many clergy/musician relationships in the church which range from 'cool' to downright pugnacious.

The time in history when the church represented wholeness (from the same root as 'holiness') seems very remote from today. For if wholeness and holiness are the same and fragmentation is their opposite, one can surely understand why today's society is being described as an increasingly secular one. Whether we speak of the many professional requirements which lay first claim on people's lives, or industries with built-in mobility for their execu-

* AMR, *Ancient and Modern Revised*; AGO, *American Guild of Organists*; WCC, *World Council of Churches*.

tives, preventing their involvement in any sort of community other than the industrial one, we are talking about fragmentation, secularization – the opposite of that which brings a wholistic experience of life to society.

Have we stopped worshipping?

What has the church to say about all this? Very little, really. The influence of the Christian church as an institution seems to be rapidly diminishing. The church would appear to have little credibility save in the area of personal morality. Does this demise signal a parallel demise of worship, a function associated so closely with the church? Are people in today's society ceasing to worship? The answer is a simple one. We can't. Having been created with this God-given ability, we are destined to be worshippers, of one sort or another. As long as we live, we human beings will keep on searching for something to fill the empty void created when sin entered between us and God. We will keep on worshipping. We want more than anything to be unified, to be whole, and we will go to any lengths to fill the emptiness we feel with something.

Frequently we make a particular interest the very centre of life without even knowing it. Ecology, politics, suburbanism, success in work . . . none of these is 'bad' in itself. Yet when exalted to a position of ultimate worth, i.e. when they become that axis around which our lives revolve, they become idols. When our whole world falls apart because of any of these things, they have surely become our idols. They have taken the place of the God who has made it clear to us – 'I am a jealous God' – that he alone can focus our lives.

What God do we really worship? The story of God's people in the Old Testament illustrates the fact that, although they were a worshipping people by nature, they were not and had never been monogamous in their worship. The Old Testament is replete with stories telling how God's people fell away from him to follow other gods. Abraham was called out of a land that served idols, and for his descendents ever since there has been a constant struggle to keep from being pulled here and there by the attraction of other gods. It was not that the people did not want to follow Yahweh, the true God; they simply wanted to bring along their other gods as well. They wanted the best of both worlds!

> *Joshua said to all the people, 'This is what the Lord, the God of Israel says: "Long ago your forefathers, including Terah the father of Abraham and Nahor, lived beyond the River and worshipped other gods. . ." Now fear the Lord and serve Him with all faithfulness. Throw away the gods your forefathers worshipped beyond the River and in Egypt, and serve the Lord. But if serving the Lord seems undesirable to you, then choose for youselves this day whom you will serve, whether the gods your forefathers served beyond the River, or the gods of the Amorites, in whose land you are living. But as for me and my household, we will serve the Lord.'*
>
> *Then the people answered, 'Far be it from us to forsake the Lord to serve other gods! It was the Lord our God himself who brought us and our forefathers up out of Egypt from that land of slavery, and performed those great signs before our eyes. He protected us on our entire journey and among all the nations through which we travelled. And the Lord drove out before us all the nations, including the*

Amorites who lived in the land. We too will serve the Lord, because he is our God.'

Joshua said to the people, 'You are not able to serve the Lord. He is a holy God. He is a jealous God. He will not forgive your rebellion and your sins. If you forsake the Lord and serve foreign gods, he will turn and bring disaster on you and make an end of you, after he has been good to you.'

But the people said to Joshua, 'No! We will serve the Lord.'

Then Joshua said, 'You are witnesses against yourselves that you have chosen to serve the Lord.'

'Yes, we are witnesses,' they replied.

'Now then,' said Joshua, 'throw away the foreign gods that are among you and yield your hearts to the Lord, the God of Israel.'

And the people said to Joshua, 'We will serve the Lord our God and obey him.' . . . Israel served the Lord throughout the lifetime of Joshua and of the elders who outlived him and who had experienced everything the Lord had done for Israel (Joshua 24:2, 14–21, 31).

This passage and many others show us the function of the prophets. They point out to God's people that they have strayed from him and are in fact worshipping other gods; they remind them of their identity as his people, recalling them to himself. Prophets both ancient and modern offer such warning signals. They know that God's people will either hate the one (their idols) and love the other (God), or they will hold to the one (their idols) and despise the other (God) (Matthew 6:24). They cannot serve God and mammon. Not now, not in Joshua's time; not ever. Small wonder that prophets in every age are far from popular.

In the twelfth century Francis of Assisi and his followers exercised a notable healing ministry. It was not unusual for the lame to throw down their crutches and walk when St Francis and his disciples passed by; many healing miracles were associated with his ministry. But, strangely, there were in Assisi some cripples who would scurry for cover and hide when St Francis entered the town. Did they not want to be healed? Why should they avoid this miraculous power, this saintly man? Perhaps they knew instinctively that their entire life would change if they were healed. No longer could they beg on the street corners; they would be whole and able to work, and play, and to be responsible for themselves. It is strange to think of a beggar's lot as being a comfortable rut, but such was the case in Assisi, it would appear.

We in our affluent Western society are really no different than the cripples in Assisi. When we hear the prophetic word of God, when he speaks to us in the depths of our being, we will have to change. When we avoid the discomfort of the prophetic word, when we scurry for cover like the cripples of Assisi, is it not because we prefer the *status quo*? Suburban living, job security, ethnic supremacy . . . the list of comforts, crutches and idols goes on and on. How easy it was in Assisi, how easy it is today, to become stuck, to be so unrecognizing of our idols that we have difficulty hearing God and moving out of our ruts to follow him. For worship to have integrity, we must identify the idols with which we struggle. We need to know not only who it is we are worshipping, but who it is we are not worshipping!

Our baptismal vows state the matter clearly. For it is there that we publicly proclaim our turning to Christ and away from his spiritual enemies. We renounce the world, the flesh, and the devil.

Q. *Do you renounce Satan and all the spiritual forces of wickedness that rebel against God?*
A. *I renounce them.*

Q. *Do you renounce the evil powers of this world
which corrupt and destroy the creatures of God?*

A. *I renounce them.*[4]

Such vows are surely no one-off thing, but the
sacramental beginning of a lifelong engagement with
these forces. In order to discern the idols we are
tempted to worship, God's people need leaders who
are themselves discerning of these spiritual enemies
and ready to renounce them. Often our spiritual foes
are subtle ones. The 'high places' of idolatry in the
Old Testament, the significance of the golden calf
seem unmistakable. But how quick are we to recognize our own idols? How about consumerism . . .
or national security . . . social success . . . family . . .
good health?

Returning to the United States after eight years in
Britain, I was unable to pick up a magazine without
being bombarded with the latest health fad, ranging
from a 'Fantastic' new diet plan to the latest exercise
craze. The fact that we, the people who buy maga-
zines, are so eager to read all of this speaks of a real
preoccupation with health. It is not simply that we
want to be healthy. Of course we do. But in an
affluent society such as the United States, leisure
time affords the pursuit of many self-improvement,
self-analysis, self-help programmes designed to
perpetuate our youth and good looks as long as possible. We can easily become worshippers at the altar
of good health and longevity.

There are certain idols which have a peculiar
propensity for curling up in church pews; they apparently feel quite at home there. There is, for example,
traditionalism ('Well, we *always*. . .' 'Yes, it is a
gigantic lectern for such a tiny church, but you see,
we could *never* move it! It was a memorial gift from
the Jones family. . .'). Or there is doctrine: ('Is he a
born-again Christian?') or church polity: ('Yes, we

allow certain women to be unofficial elders. . .').
Whether we curry favor with the wealthy, e.g. the
Jones family, or 'sloganize' our faith to the point of
erecting barriers for those on the 'outside', or fly in
the face of the Spirit's liberating activity in our age,
we need within the church those who will wave red
flags to show us the danger spots along the way. We
need worship leaders who discern the subtle idols
within the church.

Integrity in our worship

> *These people come near to me with their mouth and
> honour me with their lips, but their hearts are far
> from me. Their worship of me is made up only of rules
> taught by men' (Isaiah 29:13).*

God insists that our worship of him has integrity,
that it should not be divorced from the rest of life.
Would the God who died that we might have life
and have it more abundantly feel more at home
visiting one of our churches or going to a football
game? Various mental images flood the mind,
because we have today many sorts of churches, not
to mention the varieties of football games. But the
point is this: if it is truly the living God we worship,
we cannot possibly worship such a God with dead
services, dull sermons, and dreary music! Far better
that we stop fooling ourselves, pretending that we
can honour God by dutiful church attendance and
half-hearted participation. Far better we join the
assembly of those who are celebrating life, who are
free to sing and jump and shout and get excited
about something! Perhaps, after all, we will be much
more likely to encounter the God of life there
than in a place where life does not seem to be cele-
brated.

This point was brought home all too clearly to me
once when I met a young Scottish singer in Waterloo

Station, London. She was telling me a bit about her singing career, which took place mostly in clubs. I asked her if she ever sang in churches.

'I used to,' she said, 'but not anymore. You see, I could never tell if the people enjoyed it. They never smiled or anything. Now, in the clubs you can tell when people are enjoying it.'

'What an indictment,' I thought! What a sad picture of the church as a dour, joyless group, afraid to respond. Have we been bewitched into thinking that if we leave our humanity at the back door of the church along with our raincoats, we will somehow appear more 'holy' to God?

Undoubtedly, there are churches where this young, Scottish singer might have found a warm and appreciative hearing. Let us not forget, whoever we are and whatever our church tradition, that Jesus came to break down the wall between sacred and secular. He came to hallow life's ordinariness, and present us whole (holy) before our God and Father. When this theological truth permeates our being, we will find ourselves being set free to live in our bodies, to present them as a living sacrifice to God, and to enjoy God forever!

Integrity in living our lives

If we need integrity in the way we express our worship to God, we also need integrity in the way we live our lives. There is a Chinese proverb which describes a group of people going to a banquet. The banquet table was laden with wonderful food, but when the people approached the table their arms were stiff and they could not get the food to their mouths, no matter how hard they tried. Finally, after a period of great frustration, one of the people had a clever idea. He began to feed his sister beside him. Seeing this example, the others began to do

29

likewise, and soon they all were partaking of the banquet.

In so many ways the Lord says to us, 'He who seeks to save his life will lose it.' And again, to those whom he called blessed of his Father, he said, 'For I was hungry and you fed me.' Worship of God is incompatible with injustice to persons. We can only worship with integrity when we are also involved in seeking justice, and when we have a special regard for the poor. In an affluent society we may be sorely tempted to keep thumbing to the verses which tell us how much God wants to bless us. This 'prosperity gospel' would pile up proof-text upon proof-text to convince us that God wants his people to get blessed and blessed and more blessed, and to enjoy a tremendously abundant life while two-thirds of the world goes to bed hungry. In our day the ministry of Jesus is still one of bringing good news to the poor, and where he goes we, his disciples, follow.

Worship is not only incompatible with injustice to persons; it is also incompatible with lack of reconciliation. Sometimes we are tempted to use this truth as an escape-hatch. For example, if we are feeling out of sorts with someone we will just stay away from the service because we feel 'unworthy' or 'unprepared'. In actual fact, the discipline of corporate worship, far from offering us an easy way out, can challenge us and provide a very great motivation for reconciliation. If you are committed to gather together with God's people in a corporate act of worship and you know of someone with whom you have a strained relationship, what better time to seek to be restored in fellowship to that sister or brother?

Offering all we are to God

Clearly, if our worship is to have integrity, we are going to have to bring our whole selves, warts and all, before the Lord. Do we really believe we can offer

God all of ourselves? Are we not tempted at times to hide our real feelings and only present our 'Christian' feelings (whatever we mean by that)? Perhaps we are in a period of depression or bereavement over the loss of a loved one; we stay away from gatherings because we can't predict our own tearfulness. Yet surely the assembly of God's faithful people should be a place of healing, of comfort and solace. Were we not so concerned with outward appearances, we could get on with the very exposing and vulnerable business of presenting our bodies as a living sacrifice. Perhaps we are not thoroughly convinced that God wants every emotion brought into his presence. We can even feel embarrassed when we read the Psalms which express strong negative emotions such as revenge. It comes as an offence to our civilized exterior to hear about God bloodying the heads of his enemies or dashing their little ones against the stones. Yet if we are to be completely honest, which of us at some point in our lives has not wanted to get even – in the worst way – with someone who has wounded us?

The Psalms, running the full gamut of human experience and emotion poured out to God, offer us a glimpse into the nature of Jewish worship. For our Hebrew forebears the worship of Yahweh was a passionate affair, involving every fibre of their beings. By comparison (and suffering from comparison, I'm afraid) the typical picture of an assembly of worshipping Christians in the Western world is one of cool rationality. Ours appears to be the BIG THINK religion; a tremendous amount of time is spent sitting and listening. Nevertheless, God is still inviting us to offer him all of ourselves; let us not forget that whatever we do not offer him he cannot possibly redeem. Whatver we do offer him, however awkwardly, however embarrassingly, he will work with, he will redeem.

Therefore I urge you, in view of God's mercy, to offer your bodies as living sacrifices, holy and pleasing to God – which is your spiritual worship (Romans 12:1).

3: Building Worship Together . . .
understanding liturgy

First fruits —
bring the first fruits to the altar —
But why?
to deny ourselves?
to show our piety?
That's what we've come to think,
but turn back the clocks —
look back through the ages
to where it all began.
See the Hebrew children
gathering the cattle,
grain,
wine,
and see the procession,
the offering made,
the altar laden
and watch the celebration begin.
They knew,
those Hebrew children,
they knew it was
a tithe of thanksgiving
an offering together
of the best they had
to make a celebration
to the God who gives his people all they need.

And now we come
ages later
hesitant, reluctant, glum
or worse,

> *martyr-like, pious,*
> *to offer*
> *the least we can spare*
> *to the programmes*
> *that make us feel*
> *most worthwhile.*
> *But where are the cymbals?*
> *Where is the tambourine?*
> *And when did we forget*
> *how to sing and dance and*
> *celebrate?*
>
> *He has given us more than we need.*
> *We are children in his household.*
> *He calls us*
> *the first fruits,*
> *He is gathering us together.*
> *So let us lay ourselves*
> *on his altar,*
> *a tithe.*
> *Then light the candles,*
> *pour the wine*
> *and let the celebration begin!*
>
> 'The Tithe' by Jodi Page Clark

What is liturgy?

Recently I visited the seaside resort town of Galveston, Texas, for a celebration in which it seemed everyone took part. A few years earlier, an old sailing ship, the *Elissa*, had been discovered by an American marine archeologist travelling in Greece. Built in Aberdeen in 1877, she had had a career of more than ninety years in sea-borne trade, sailing the Atlantic regularly, but soon reaching out to India, Burma and Australia. More recently she had been motorized, had fallen into the hands of smugglers, and at the time of her discovery was a sad remains of her former glory. The American traveller caught a vision of a restored *Elissa*. But who would pay the bill for such an undertaking? Borrowing money and using his own schooner as security, he bought her.

Then began the long search for the support needed to have her restored. Finally the Galveston Historical Foundation took up the challenge, had her repaired and towed across the Atlantic, where a host of skills (of the sort needed in the vanishing craft of building sailing ships) were assembled from near and far. Also, much time and labour were donated by townspeople in Galveston. Over a three-year period and at a cost of one million dollars the ship came to life again.

On the day of her official dedication she was a wonder to behold, with her polished decks and billowing white sails against an azure sky. A great celebration was planned. The whole town turned out. There was champagne for all! Entertainment included authentic Scottish folk music; the air was filled with the pungent strains of bagpipes, reminding us nostalgically of the ship's origin centuries ago in Aberdeen on the Scottish coast. *A liturgy.* And why? The original meaning of the word liturgy is 'a public work done at private cost'. The Galveston event captures the essence of it, I believe. Now schoolchildren and other visitors to Galveston Island can tour an authentic sailing ship, a present reminder to our mass production mentality of the beauty and skill involved in craftsmanship. Because of the generosity and hard work of a few – on behalf of the larger community – she stands as a proud link with the past. *A liturgy.*

Historic roots of the word 'liturgy'

Liturgy has two important aspects: people and work. The Greek words *laos* (People) and *ergon* (work) constitute the roots of our English word *liturgy*. and, as we have seen, the original usage was within the

35

context of private cost and public benefit. Seen in this way, Christ's life of obedience and death on the cross is a liturgy *par excellence*: a public work done at extreme personal cost, and in view of all. When he hung on the cross of Calvary, he made a public demonstration of the love of God, the likes of which had never been seen before or since. As the old hymn puts it,

> *There was no other good enough*
> *to pay the price of sin,*
> *He only could unlock the gate*
> *Of heav'n, and let us in.*[2]

There was a price to be paid; he paid it. He let us in. And ever since, his disciples have seen their own lives as participating in the liturgy of his life. St Paul tells the Philippians,

> . . . *even if I am being poured out like a drink-offering on the sacrifice and service coming from your faith, I am glad and rejoice with all of you (Phi. 2:17).*

Here the Greek text reads literally, '. . . if my life is poured out on the sacrifice and liturgy of your faith. . .' As we follow in the apostolic tradition today, we need an acute awareness that at the root of all public worship in the Christian church is this concept of lives poured out that all may be 'brought in'. Do we seek to please ourselves? This is not liturgy. Do we cling to our traditions as to a bobbing bark in a storm-tossed sea? This is not liturgy. Liturgy is ever re-defining itself in the lives of those who are gathered, and giving, in order that all may receive.

Distinguishing between worship and liturgy

Liturgy is the people's work. It is quite distinct from worship, the broader word which encompasses all

36

that we are, offered to God moment by moment as we live out our lives. Liturgy is a stylized summary of all that we mean by worship. Obviously, a worship service cannot include all that we mean by worship, so it is necessary to find a way to represent this reality in a form which is succinct. Liturgy does this. Good liturgy does it successfully, and people come away from a gathering of God's people satisfied, fulfilled. An analogy may be helpful here: There is a difference between being thankful and actually saying, 'thank you' to someone to whom you feel thankful! Or consider another analogy: you can love someone and know that you love them, yet something happens when you say, 'I love you'. Taking the time, finding the occasion to express this love not only communicates the reality to the other person; it strengthens the bond and makes the reality of the love stronger. So with liturgy. There is a difference between the soul's sincere desire, and the gathered praises of God's people. There is a difference between the continual offering to God of worship by his people in various times and places and circumstances, and the 'doing of it together' as corporate worship – a fulfilling summary of all our little 'worships', of all that we are and all that he is to us.

Jesus' own example of participation in the common worship practices of the synagogue speaks clearly of his valuing the liturgical process. He read lessons (Luke 4:18). He submitted himself to baptism; '. . . for it is proper for us to do this to fulfill all righteousness' (Matt. 3:13–15). His was in no sense a private religion, content with pietism; it was a life of obedience to God lived out in full view of, in submission to (and often in conflict with) the religious institutions of his day. A careful reading of Paul's epistles reveals how the Apostle was greatly concerned with the ordering of worship in the churches under his charge. He spoke to the Corinthians of their preparation for corporate worship. 'When you come together, everyone has a hymn, or a word of instruction, a revelation, a tongue or an interpretation. All of these must be done for the strengthening of the church' (I Cor. 14:26). Then he proceeded to advise them about the good order of such an assembly. From the verses which follow it is clear that not everything that everyone 'has' will be offered at one meeting. For example, he counsels them to limit prophetic utterances to 'two or three,' and concludes the various points of his instruction to them with the words, 'For God is not a god of disorder but of peace.' What *is* clear is that the people of God are responsible for the content of their corporate worship. Everyone has a gift to bring, a contribution to make, whether it be given overt hearing or remains a hidden part of the prayerful fabric of the gathering. Everyone has. There is not one ungifted person in our midst.

Perspectives for today's liturgy

Liturgy is the people's work, in St Paul's day, in our own time, always. Having considered briefly some of the historic roots and applications of the word, let us turn to today's usage and peculiar problems. What is our contemporary world like, and what are some of the concerns that we have as we enter into planning our liturgies and exercising our worship leadership roles in today's church? We will look at some perspectives for contemporary liturgy.

The need to simplify

In the last decade there has been a great proliferation of materials for worship. There are a host of new hymnals, new liturgies being published, not to mention the less official but very popular songbooks with new music aimed at the worshipping church. All of these combine to offer us flexibility in shaping worship services. Considering the fact that the liturgical reforms are so widespread and revolutionary (until 1980 when the *Alternative Service Book* was published the Church of England had not had a major change in its common prayer practices since 1662), it is small wonder that such an array of complementary materials is needed to facilitate the new liturgies. Also, the complexity of today's society begs an approach to liturgy which is far from simplistic. Our materials for worship must encompass and speak to the complexity. So it would be foolish in the extreme for a church today to oversimplify by limiting its resources to a narrow range (e.g. one hymnal only).

Still, there are attendant and very great problems in the practical use of these worship aids. It is easy to get lost when shuffling too many books! Or you can get quite confused when turning back and forth to various pages trying to take advantage of all the options offered. Clearly, we need some guidelines in the use of the new resources. How can we help make things simpler for our congregations? I would like to suggest several ways.

First, we can make use of the phenomenon of folk leadership which has thoroughly permeated Roman Catholic worship since Vatican II. The 'folk leader' in a contemporary Roman Catholic mass is the visible leader of the congregation in their responses during the Mass. The musical portions alloted to the congregation are rudimentary, easy to sing and simple to follow, if there is an encouraging lead. A gifted folk leader can accomplish much with very little. Characteristic of this style of leadership are: (a) visibility (this person must be seen in order to be followed); (b) presence (a troubadour quality which makes it easy for this person to gather others into song); (c) a strong singing voice and a convincing rhythmic technique, frequently associated with the guitar, for indicating the 'beat' and providing an accompaniment to the singing. All in all, the 'picture' is worth a thousand words!

Another means of simplifying our services is by the use of a thoughtfully prepared order of service which functions as a guide. This is particularly beneficial if you want to use song resources from several books and hymnals, yet do not wish to burden people with too many books. Obviously, someone will need to bear the burden of investigating copyright procedures, even for the printing of words. And here the temptation is to immediate discouragement. The average person can feel overwhelmed at the prospect of asking permission for every song that is printed. However, there is no substitute for getting one's feet wet in the matter. All that is required is one faithful soul who has a concern for making new resources available in your church, and who is not afraid of writing letters and asking questions!

You will soon discover that many of the songs you wish to use are the copyright of just a handful of publishers. You will also discover that groupings of songs from one publisher may be used over a period of time, e.g. a calendar year, for a nominal fee. Some publishers will require no fee for the printing of words only, but simply an acknowledgement of the copyright. The temptation to criticize those who collect, edit, copy, proof-read, arrange, copy, proof-read again, print and publish music should be resisted!

It is, in fact, quite erroneous to assume that paying for the music we use in our churches is a new phenomenon. We have always paid for it. A quick glance at any hymnal will show a list of copyright holders, each of whom may have received royalties for the inclusion of their words or music. The cost of each hymnal covers such necessary expenses as the payment of royalties. Obviously, if you are putting together a tailor-made songsheet, the responsibility for such administrative details moves much closer to home. But it is by no means an imponderable task.

Letters of inquiry to copyright holders should state clearly:

1. *the title and composer of the song*
2. *what you intend to print (words, or words and melody, or words and full music score)*
3. *how many copies you intend printing*
4. *the nature of the printed matter (songsheet, weekly order-of-service, special one-time use, as, for example, a conference songsheet)*
5. *whether the usage is commercial or non-commercial (i.e., will it be for sale?)*

Still another visual aid and means of simplification in our contemporary liturgies is the use of a large white board with different colours to indicate the various books or sheets to be used in the service, e.g., red for the traditional hymnal, blue for the service book, green for the contemporary songbook. Over a period of time people can become helpfully conditioned to the use of colour coding, and the white boards are easy to use, wiping clean with a cloth and not needing to be washed (as are blackboards which, more often than not, turn out to be tattle-tale grey!) The bright colours look very cheerful, and provided you have a good scribe, the overall effect is neat and attractive. Coloured numbers also work well on traditional hymnboards.

A simple printed order of service can facilitate the use of materials from several songbooks. The words to the songs may be printed on economically-priced paper (probably using a mimegraph stencil). The great advantage in this approach is that congre-

41

gations are then not limited to one, two or even three books, but can be free to draw from a wide range of resources, provided of course that someone has done the necessary homework on the copyright requirements. The music director should take care to write or type out the words for the person who will do the typing of the stencil. There are ways and there are ways to print words, and the most obvious will not always be the most helpful to a singing congregation. In printing the refrain of this song:

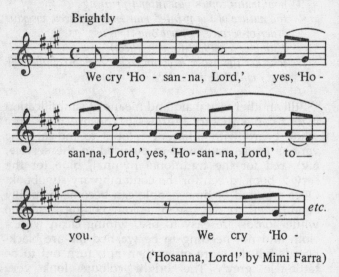

('Hosanna, Lord!' by Mimi Farra)

Setting out the words as follows:

We cry 'Hosanna, Lord,' yes, 'Hosanna, Lord,' yes, 'Hosanna, Lord' to you. (Repeat).

certainly saves space, but it does not give the feel for the musical phrase which this version does:

42

We cry, 'Hosanna, Lord,'
yes, 'Hosanna, Lord,'
yes, 'Hosanna, Lord' to you.
(Repeat)

Remember: the means is the message

Probably the least effective but curiously the most widely used tool for simplification is peppering the service with verbal instructions. Too many instructions along the way inevitably spoil the flow of good liturgy. Do this, turn to that, now we are going to . . . sit down, stand up. . .! If we are not careful we can turn our liturgy into a subliminal classroom – a place where everyone is waiting to be told what to do next. It is far better to give a few instructions at the outset and rely on one or more of the visual aids afore-mentioned to guide us through! Congregations can take much more responsibility along these lines than we sometimes give them credit for. Another good rule of thumb for those conducting services is: never say with words what you can say with a simple movement. For example, a graceful upward movement of the arms with palms up will say 'Now it's time to stand' without attracting attention to the mechanics of standing or interrupting the flow of the liturgy.

The means is the message. Using the *means* of instructional words communicates the *message* that we are at school, even though the worst offenders at this sort of thing would be horrified to find out that they had effectively turned their churches into schoolrooms! We may have selected very carefully what we think the message or content of our service will be, but if the means by which we lead the congregation through it is not equally and as thoughtfully prepared, we will miss the boat – the worship boat, that is. Perhaps the choir has learned a too-ambitious anthem for the Bishop's annual visitation. We may think the message is, 'High praise to God (just look, we're singing our most ambitious anthem!)' when really the message coming across to the person in the pew is, 'Jiminy Cricket!! Will they make it?' Or, we may think, 'This is going to be a wonderful service; we have such an exciting assortment of music!' when really the people are feeling like: 'Fuss and bother! There are too many books. Help! Now what?'

Is the music suitable?

Clearly, if we want the real message to get across, the means must be carefully chosen. Pope Paul VI has given us a valuable keyword in the selection of music for use in the liturgy: that of suitability. If we are to select music that is suitable, then we must, first of all, know how music functions in the context of corporate worship. There are two ways. First, it helps to preserve the corporate memory of our faith and our tradition. In a single phrase from a hymn a whole panorama of Biblical history can be brought before our eyes: 'The God of Abraham praise' recalls to us the saga of Abraham's life, and simultaneously the sturdy strains of *Leoni* strengthen our perception of the father of faith. The great hymns of Christendom have a wonderful way of preserving the corporate memory of our faith. Secondly, music stimulates our deepest emotions. It bypasses our intellect, and gets to the heart of the matter – us. It reaches us at the level of our feelings, going directly to the intuitive part of our brain. 'Candy is dandy, but liquor is quicker!', said Ogden Nash.[3] Music is able to reach us where words can't. And this fact bring with it some definite implications: we must be sure that the music we choose matches the words. If the music and words don't match, the words will inevitably suffer and get lost in the shuffle, but we will remember the music. A humorous example may help:

As a tango (♩ = 116)

Praise God from whom all bless-ings flow; Praise him, all crea - tures here be - low; Praise him a - bove, ye heav'n-ly host; Praise Fa - ther Son and Ho-ly Ghost. A - men!

('Hernando's Hideaway' from The Pajama Game by R. Adler & J. Ross)

The torrid strains of a song such as 'Hernando's Hideaway' will be remembered long after the words of the Doxology have faded away. This should give us food for thought. The chief function of music in the context of worship is to enhance the word, and the mood of the hymn (i.e. the words) governs the suitability of the tune, '. . . for the enormous power that the tune has of enforcing or even creating a mood is the one invaluable thing of magnitude which overrides every other consideration.'[4]

The music we choose should suit the part of the service in which it is used, as well as relating to the broader concerns of special seasons and themes. 'O Come, all ye faithful' is a wonderful welcome to a service, but its Christmas connotations are so strong that we would do well to think carefully before scheduling it on a Sunday in July. 'Jesus took my burdens' is a compelling little chorus for a service of prayer and praise, but let's not sing it as the children are going out to their class, lest they take it personally! Our concern to amplify a particular theme or season must not violate the integrity of a single worship event. Frequently, in our attempts to have a cohesive service, we catch 'theme-itis', a disease characterized by trying to relate every hymn to the theme for the day. We need not cling desperately to the appointed Scripture readings to provide the 'meat' for our liturgical meal, from which we take our cue in selecting the vegetables and salad to serve. It may be Lent and repentance our theme, but if I am greeted at the church door with 'Turn Back, o man' the church door may be as far as I get!

The community as celebrant

Let's consider the Eucharist or communion service as a point of reference. Far from needing a theme to give it substance, the liturgy itself, deriving its whole content from the word of God, is meat indeed. It has its own shape and makes its own requirements. In the creative process the artist takes hold of a work, but ultimately the work takes hold of the artist. So it is in liturgy: we take hold of planning a service but sooner or later the service begins to speak to us and to make its own demands (if we are listening.) Artistic and liturgical integrity have that in common.

46

Writing about *Sacagawea*, his famous piece of sculpture, Harry Jackson said:

> *I'm just finishing her off. The overall simple statement is still there I hope. But really one can never know when one is in the work and letting it lead along only God knows where. The way to make a work of art is the way to ride an unknown horse, that likely will be more than you've ever straddled; just take a deep seat, don't look sideways, keep your mind in the middle and the forked end down. Anything else will bring the ride or the work of art to nothing.*[5]

Planning liturgies for the contemporary church is every bit as challenging, the ride can be very bumpy at times, and the Holy Spirit may seem like more of a horse than we had bargained for! Recalling that the liturgy is the community's action will help us keep our 'forked end down' and save us from 'theme-itis' (or using corporate worship to get our points across.) The adventure is there for the taking!

4: When we gather . . . more about liturgy

It was Palm Sunday and we were gathering together for a parish Eucharist. Upon entering the church, young and old alike were handed a slender palm frond (not the usual ready-made palm crosses.) After the processional hymn the plan unfolded: we were to make our own palm crosses, following three easy steps. A teacher from the Sunday school stood in front of the congregation and carefully demonstrated the procedure for folding the frond and weaving it into a cross. It looked simple enough – until we began the process. Then it suddenly seemed harder. As the moments passed, a few chuckles could be heard in the midst of our intense concentration. People began to steal embarrassed glances at their neighbours' handiwork. Only the younger children dared hold theirs up for others to see. (In desperation I resorted to a paper clip to keep mine together.) By the time the celebrant rose, things were in a mild state of confusion.

A prayer was to follow, blessing the crosses. The celebrant stood, grinned sheepishly and said, 'What shall we pray? "God bless this mess!!" ' Whereupon we all were set free to laugh. And in a strange and totally unexpected way, we were drawn close together.

Good liturgy gives expression to the reality of the moment. We would do well, then, to consider just what we are about as we go through the various parts of a service. First, there is the process of gathering. It begins '. . . when the first person enters, and grows clearer and stronger as others come – *if* that person and those who follow make room for one another and make one another welcome. Only in this way will they become a community rather than a crowd of individuals.'[1] Surely then, the ministry of hospitality must be exercised as a prime requirement for beginning a service. People must become aware of one another's presence and of the significance of this moment in time. They are together forming a celebrating community which is absolutely unique: it is an unrepeatable event in history. How we greet one another as we enter is important; how the minister/celebrant interacts with the gathered people and welcomes them is important; and certainly the opening hymn must play its part in bringing everyone into the presence of God through self-awareness as his gathered people.

Next we have the process of listening. Here, through the Liturgy of the Word, the assembly is brought into a place of hearing God speak. The community of faith opens its treasure-trove of stories and images recalled through the proclamation of the Scriptures. The community retells its family history, strengthening itself for the future. Some services may contain only one lesson from Holy Scriptures, but in the Eucharist we have the potential for a veritable feast, beginning with an Old Testament reading and continuing with an Epistle and the Gospel. The rhythm of reading-response in song, reading-response in song, builds to a climax – the proclamation of the Gospel. Thus the 'Liturgy of the Word' forms a dramatic unit. Although we may at times opt for the convenience of having one reader read all the lessons, we will miss a perfect opportunity to symbolize the worshipping family by choosing readers representative of its scope, e.g. a man, a woman, a young person. Our response in song will include appropriate hymns and hopefully a Psalm.

We would do well to imitate the early Christians in our singing of the Psalms, i.e. to select those settings which feature a simple antiphon; the antiphon captures the spirit of the Psalm and can easily be sung by the congregation even if they have never heard it before. The verses of such settings are intended to be sung by a cantor (choir, folk leader or folk group.) In place of singing, the antiphonal reading of Psalms by the congregation is almost certain to be practicable. The reading of the lessons themselves needs to focus us firmly on the word of God; they are not intended to be 'dramatic readings' which send us away raving about the theatrical abilities of the reader, nor are they to be droned as if the reader had to bury his own personality in order to sound 'holy'. Canon Joseph Poole, an eminent liturgist in the Church of England, has given us a wonderful description of how the Bible is/could be read in a service of worship. . .

Imagine the situation. Many members of the congregation, it may be, have come for the music, not for the message (for of course the service does carry a message). So some of them may be thinking, 'A bit from the Bible? A bit from the Bible already? What a bore!'

A bore it may be; but if it's a bore that will not be the Bible's fault; it will be yours. Perhaps the people can't hear clearly what you are reading; more likely they can hear well enough, but you don't make them want to listen because you use the wrong kind of voice, a boring, dull voice, a churchy voice. Don't sound churchy: sound secular, sound human, sound happy!

You are at home, rehearsing the lesson you are to read in church. There is a friend in the room with you – or perhaps there is nobody with you. No matter; pick up today's newspaper, look it over, and choose out from the news (not from a leading article) a passage of

three short paragraphs. Then say out loud: 'I say!
Listen to this! Two hooded men broke into a bank in
the high street' (or whatever you've chosen to read
out.) Finish the passage; then, without the least change
in your manner or your tone of voice , go straight
into the lesson. You will find yourself automatically
sounding secular and sounding human, even while
you are reading the Bible. This trick of the trade has
never been known to fail. Give it a try.[2]

Following the process of gathering and the process
of listening there is the process of sharing. In the
Eucharist this takes the form of a ritual meal in which
Jesus' own last meal with his disciples is the model.
Christ is the host. The table is set for the communal
meal, the food and drink are presented, we offer
thanks to the Father for his gifts in the Eucharistic
Prayer (where, in the new liturgies, there is ample
opportunity for congregational participation), then
we break the bread and share the meal. Again, there
is opportunity for members of the worshipping
community to assist in serving the meal. And the
music chosen for use during the Communion should
strengthen the corporate nature of this event. Here
is the ideal time to sing songs with familiar refrains
for the congregation, and to avoid wordiness. In a
non-Eucharistic service the element of sharing is no
less important, although obviously it must take
different forms: a time of testimony or of open prayer
may enable us to break the bread of life together.
However it happens, we will know that God has met
with us, that we have supped with him.

Now we are ready for the process of departing.
We have been strengthened to go forth in the name
of Christ. As the Lord gathered us initially in this
rite, he will now scatter us according to his kingdom's
purpose. To go forth implies being sent; it implies
mission. To go forth in the name of Christ means to

be a Christ-bearer, a person who is happy to be known by his name. When we are scattered 'in his name' we do not suddenly revert to an individualistic mode of being. Jesus said, 'You (plural) are the light of the world'. When we go forth we go as a people, the people of God. The music we choose here must be full of hope for the redemptive work God wants to do in his world; it must see through the eyes of faith his increasing reign, his kingdom coming. And, as we go, we must know that by the grace of God we are co-workers with him. Our work is cut out for us. *Thy kingdom come, thy will be done on earth. . .*

Now, all these processes are woven into one living reality in the midst of liturgical action. Concerning the shape of the liturgy, Roland Walls says, 'God's movement isn't great chunks of stuff, it flows! It flows like our life must flow, outward and upward. The Spirit always eases things up and makes them flow.'[3] Music may be likened to the bicycle on which the liturgy rides (i.e. flows). If the music sags and lacks buoyancy, it is as if the bicycle has a flat tyre. Or, if music takes over the service, we may feel that we are riding a runaway bike with no braking power! I have visited a few churches where music seemed to be the tail that wagged the dog. It took over, and in so doing it lost its real ability to oil the machinery of the liturgy and help it move along. Good liturgy has to do with flow.

Consider the needs and abilities of the people

Pope Paul VI's axiom for good liturgical use of music includes suitability not only to the particular service we are planning and to the season in which it falls, but suitability to the needs and abilities of those taking part.

> *If Christian worship is really a symbolic activity in which an assembly expresses its faith, then it follows*

that any singing should belong to the believing people as a whole, and not be the special preserve of a few, whether they be clerics or musicians.[4]

The music of the church belongs to the people; they are the celebrants. The believing people as a whole come in many different shapes and sizes, represent at least three generations and in many cases today (the urban church being a good example) a poly-ethnic background. How shall we meet the needs of very young children, teenagers, young couples, the middle-aged, and octogenarians in the same service? Certainly where music is concerned we must purpose to be eclectic, choosing music from many and varied sources, old and new. We must not get stuck in a tiny framework, using one style or type of music.

Provost Alan Warren tells the story of a young Christian teacher who is an avid jazz fan. He now worships only at early morning services, not because he enjoys getting up early or wishes to avoid the main congregation but because 'I don't like hymns and organs and I just can't seem to worship properly with all that dull music around me.' Clearly we could pull in hundreds of opposite points of view, people who are classical music fans, and who are quite content with preludes by Bach, Tudor anthems, and hymns published around the turn of the century. If we organize ourselves according to the standards of the world around us we will put the jazz-freaks in one camp or club, and the classical-freaks in another. Then they will live happily ever after! After all, birds of a feather do flock together. What we will not have is that diversified, many-splendoured thing called variously the assembly of God's people, the family of God, the church of Jesus Christ. How many ordinary families do you know who have exactly the same taste in the music they like to hear? Not many, I daresay, if the family contains a teenager! Yet ordinary families find creative ways to cope with the problem, and certainly we are called to exercise creativity in the family which is the church.

The place in which we worship is one of the factors determining what is suitable. The hymn tempo which is suitable in a large cathedral with a six-second delay will not be suitable in a small mission church with a congregation of thirty. In the same way, the guitar can serve brilliantly as an accompanying instrument in this same small church, but will not be able, on its own, to function well in a large cathedral setting. This does not mean that folk instruments can never be used successfully in larger buildings, but it does mean that an adequate sound system is needed.

Do we need a liturgy group

How can we possibly deal with the multitude of considerations which boggle the mind when one begins to think of meeting the needs of diverse, mobile congregations? Perhaps a good place to begin would be with the people themselves; it could be illuminating to hear in some sort of forum how they actually *feel* about the church's worship life. Such a forum could give needed reinforcement to 'the people's work' of liturgy, especially in churches where 'they' (the professional clergy and musicians) do all the planning. One possible by-product of such a forum might be the discovery of men and women who have particular insights into the whole worship question, who have a certain charisma in this area. Many churches today are forming liturgy groups in which the ordained minister and professional musician can have access to other gifted members of their church.

Such groups can provide a listening ear, a barometer of the pastoral climate of the worshipping body. Their most valuable contribution is not in the finely detailed planning of the services week by week, but rather in looking at the broader picture. Perhaps an entire season of the church's life needs to be examined. Ask yourselves, 'How shall we, as a church family, celebrate Advent this year?' Perhaps change is indicated. You may ask yourselves, 'How can we make the beginning of the service more compelling so as to encourage punctuality?' Perhaps our services are too long to engage the children present (even some of the adults!) and we need reminding that the mind cannot comprehend what the seat cannot endure. Or we may belong to a 'renewed' church where services have become so friendly that we lack any sense of corporate repose, of being able to be gracefully quiet together, creating holy expectancy.

Where shall the world be found, where will the word resound? Not here, there is not enough silence![5]

Whatever our case may be, a corporate caring for the quality of our liturgical life will bear fruit; it may well be one of the keys to learning about building worship together.

5: Simple is Beautiful . . . the church's folk music

Is music the 'war department' in your church? 'Why does he always play the hymns like a dirge?' 'No, I go at eleven; I simply can't bear it when they use guitars.' There is in the church today a discernible tension between predictability and spontaneity, between tradition and innovation, between the professional – clergyman or musician – who represents the stream of tradition in the church, and the ministrel or wandering troubadour who is in touch with the popular imagination. The former stands for good order and a structural link with the past; the latter has a gift of communication, of simple poetry and song to reflect life's changing circumstances. The late Eric Routley in his book *Music Leadership in the Church* describes this tension as a healthy one, one which has been with us through the ages.

> *On the one hand, it is accepted, in the prophetic tradition of song, that sacred music is something ecstatic, inspired, topical; it is associated with dancing and with a kind of high intoxication with religion; its great symbolic figures are the flawed genius of Israel's ambition, and David, the adventurer-king of Israel's glory. Sacred music has its roots in human life with all its tragedy and all its brilliance – in Saul the beautiful and Saul the insane, in David the serene young singer who could cast out Saul's devils . . . and in David the arrogant autocrat who shamed himself with Bathsheba. (And think also of the implications of David calming Saul's frenzy with music, and of Saul*

later saying, "I'll stick him to the wall with my spear if he won't give over playing that guitar.") That is one tradition of sacred music.

The other is the tradition of order and liturgy, the tradition of Levi and Asaph and Heman – of men who are merely names in the biblical records. What do any of us know of Levi and Asaph, compared with what we know of Saul? Here is impersonal, legislative, liturgical music. Here is music full of religious joy and splendour, no doubt, but professional, tamed, **sacred**. *Its genius is not in common life but in the holiness, the separateness, of worship.*[1]

So there is a strong line of sacred music which may be described as 'ecstatic', 'inspired', God's gift for the moment. And there is an equally strong tradition of order and liturgy through the Levites, who had charge of the tabernacle of the Lord. These two traditions have existed side by side throughout the history of God's people.

And what is the situation today? Are these two strains of our common Judeo-Christian heritage integrated in the church? An analogy from the business world may prove helpful. Think of a company with great administrators but no innovators. It will soon be over-shadowed by more imaginative companies. Conversely, a company with gifted innovators and weak administration may soon end in bankruptcy! (Too many bright ideas!) The twentieth century church very much needs all of the enabling gifts to be functioning within the local body of Christ. We need our liturgists and priests who are anchored in a strong sense of history. We also need our prophets, our innovators/folk artists who can express old truths in new forms. We need good order and spontaneity – not one or the other – if we are to be truly catholic, embracing the length and breadth of our biblical history.

Folk art communicates ancient truths in a language understood by all; by virtue of that fact, and because it is a faithful reflection of the mood, feelings, and concerns of the people themselves, it is of the essence of the church's expression of worship. To clarify the meaning of folk art, I would like to draw some comparisons between it and what is called *fine art*.

Who creates it?

If I play this famous quotation for you:

your response is likely to be immediate, and almost certain to be 'Beethoven'! (Some of you will pin it down even more, Beethoven's Fifth Symphony in C minor!) We associate this very famous theme with an equally famous composer. Now if I play this:

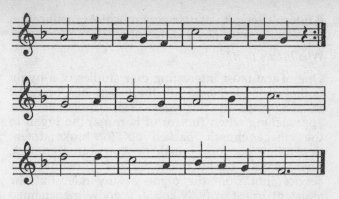

the response may well be a long silence or a shrug of the shoulders. The person who wrote this familiar and well-loved tune seems to have been lost in the stream of history; this person has not been immortalized as was Beethoven. The fact is that we haven't the faintest idea who wrote this tune. it is a folk tune. And even if we did know, we would not be likely to recognize the person's name. Look at random through the index of composers and musical sources in any hymnal and you will find an assortment of basically unknown names: Johann Rudolph Ahle, Arthur Henry Mann, Ithamar Conkey. . . (certainly none of them in a league with Beethoven!) Or you will find simply the statement 'Composer unknown,' or 'Traditional Dutch', or the name of a person or place somehow associated with the history and use of the hymn (e.g. 'Rockingham', 'Deidre', 'Duke Street'). And there we see a fundamental difference between folk art and fine art. The composer of 'fine art' is likely to be a celebrity, and the work is associated very closely with the person who wrote it. Not so with folk art. Think of the hundreds of hymns you know: you may recognize the text as being Wesley, or Watts, but the music? Most of it was written by relatively unknown people, and interestingly enough, it doesn't seem to matter very much! Authentication of folk art comes along different lines.

Who listens to it?

One of the most interesting case studies of a hymn is that of 'Stille Nacht'. In the village of Oberndorf in Germany, in the year 1818, Christmas was approaching when (horror of horrors!) the organ in the village church 'packed up' (or broke down, depending on your British or American leanings). There would be no music for the Christmas Eve service, not from the organ at any rate. But the assistant priest at St Nikola's, a godly man named Joseph Mohr, wrote a beautiful Christmas poem and asked his friend Franz Gruber, the church organist, to set it to music. Gruber did so, and the two of them sang 'Silent night, holy night' as a simple duet with guitar accompaniment, on Christmas Eve.

You can stand back and marvel at the story from several angles. I don't know which is the more remarkable: that an organist would be caught playing a guitar in church, or that the organist and clergyman were so in harmony with one another that they could give the church this lovely hymn as the fruit of their relationship! But there is more to the story. The organ tuner showed up some time in May, and Mohr and Gruber showed their song to him. He in turn took it back to Leipzig and promptly forgot about it for several years. But several years later he rediscovered the crumpled manuscript and showed it to some friends. Eventually the song came to the attention of a family named Strasser, who were glove makers. The Strasser daughters had lovely voices, and sang the song in the family's booth at the Leipzig Fair. A fair of all places! A place where people go simply to enjoy themselves. It was in the secular setting of a fairground that 'Stille Nacht' became popularized. People found themselves humming the tune; they liked the melody, they enjoyed the song. It had a direct simplicity about it which communicated to them. Only after this process of popularization was the song published. Only after a secular audience authenticated it did it find its way into the church as a hymn.

It is interesting to compare the original version to that which appears in most hymnals:

Even a cursory glance will tell you that today's four-part hymn (overleaf) was yesterday's folk song. It is curious how we seem to have homogenized our sacred hymn literature into such uniformity that a random page of a hymnal looks remarkably like any other page! This dulling uniformity of presentation can successfully conceal the folk origins of many hymns.

(v.2) Si - lent night, Ho - ly night,

Shep-herds quake at the sight, *etc.*

A quick look at 'Stille Nacht' shows us that the audience for folk art is a popular one. By comparison, a tutored or educated ear is necessary for a full appreciation of fine art. If I were to play for you a movement from a Bartok string quartet, some of you would be puzzled, or perhaps even stop up your ears and say 'turn it off!' Others would think it was great! The difference: an educated ear, or knowing what to listen for. Without preparation, one can be highly confused or just plain bored by fine art.

Who performs it?

Some years ago when the Community of Celebration was newly in residence at Yeldall Manor in Berkshire, a group of us drove to Windsor on a Sunday afternoon to attend Choral Evensong in St George's Chapel. We arrived early enough to be seated in the choir area, where it all happens. Seated next to me was my son David (aged 6) and next to him a young Englishman and zealous Christian named Mark, who lived with us at the time. Mark had attended Eton, so he was very familiar with the changed Psalms and canticles, but being of very ordinary musical skills, he knew the melody only. As the choir began to chant the Psalms (an impeccable four-part harmony), Mark, who was, as I have already said, a zealous sort, began to sing the melody lustily. Feeling uncomfortable, I stole a glance over my right shoulder and down the row to the stalls where the choir was seated. Sure enough! One of the section leaders in the choir was staring hard in our direction. The unspoken message was clear: as far as the choir at St George's was concerned, this kind of participation was simply 'not on'. Being a trained musician who could empathize with, indeed admire, the choir's aesthetic standards, I was growing more uncomfortable by the minute as Mark continued to sing. At that moment, with no prompting from anyone and as an absolute answer to prayer, young David nudged Mark in the ribs, and whispered, 'You're not s'posed to sing!' Mark complied without appearing to feel at all put down. Evensong continued its serene and beautiful course and my thanksgiving rose like incense!

This experience has remained with me and serves to point out yet another comparison between fine art and folk art. The choir at St George's did not expect visitors to participate in the chanting of the Psalms. Indeed, they preferred that they should not do so. And in this regard, they are no different than a performing orchestra or choral society, neither of which would expect you, as a member of the audience, to help them out. In 'fine art' there is a very clear distinction between audience and performer. 'Folk art' is of its very nature participatory, and the lines between performer and audience are much greyer. The 'audience' is invited in, either by use of a 'lining-out' technique (where the folk leader sings a phrase and the people repeat it) or by the fact of built-in repetition in the music which makes it easy to join in.

There is a quality of immediacy and accessibility in folk music that encourages a high degree of participation. Mary Travers (of *Peter, Paul and Mary*) puts it this way:

> *Folk music . . . is not a passive music; it's*
> *participatory. At a classical concert, you're not asked*
> *to participate physically, only on a mental level. It*
> *either moves you or puts you to sleep, but it does it*
> *to you singularly . . . folk music doesn't segregate age*
> *groups. There are four generations at our concerts –*
> *and all are singing.'*[2]

What purpose does it serve?

Clearly, fine art has its own 'Hall of Fame' and the pictures are hung there only after the most intense scrutiny by experts in the field. There are many aesthetic yardsticks which may be applied to a work of fine art, but the yardsticks all point in the same direction; towards a standard of excellence which is external and which judges the passing artists who dare to make their work public. Training and craftsmanship are presumed; the work of a 'Beethoven' must needs be compared to that of his contemporaries because the professional artists are all on the same ladder.

The purpose of folk art is different. Simply stated, folk art is created for the enrichment of community life: nothing more or less. In the case of 'Stille Nacht,' there was a need felt in the worshipping community, the village church in Oberndorf, for music to enrich the community's celebration of Christmas. The priest and church musician worked together to meet that need. In so doing they fulfilled the purpose of folk art. In years to come a great furore would be raised as to the worthiness of their simple song, when set alongside the work of great composers.

Professors of Music, organists, orchestra leaders, composers, lexicographers, writers, literary bigwigs and long-nosed bigots joined in the fray throughout Germany and Austria denigrating the efforts of two unpretentious men who had not profited by so much as a single sou, who had never asked for anything and who never pretended that they had done anything than the best they could at a particular minor crisis in their lives. (The only ones who loved what they had wrought, whole-heartedly and unreservedly, were people. And they numbered millions.)[3]

An English friend and critic who reviewed my composition, *The King of Glory Setting for Holy Communion* stated, 'This setting sounds as if it were written for a guitarist who knew only three chords.' His comment is very close to the truth, although my folk guitarist friends normally know at least five! The setting was indeed written for a parish where there were a number of gifted young folk singers and guitarists. There was also an organ, and there were many older people, the traditional hymn-loving sort. I set about writing a Communion setting that would help integrate these elements musically, one which would draw the worshipping community together. I envisioned a full-bodied, twelve-string guitar sound giving rhythmic thrust to the harmonic offering of the organ and keeping the latter from sounding too sombre! I intentionally limited myself to a small harmonic vocabulary (as did Gruber when he wrote 'Stille Nacht' with guitar) because of the idiomatic demands of the instrument. The whole purpose of the exercise was what? To please the critics? No, the setting was written for one purpose only: to enrich the life of that community. Such is the purpose of all folk art.

	FOLK ART	FINE ART
composer	frequently unknown	celebrity
audience	popular	refined
participation	large degree of participation	clear distinction between artist and audience
purpose	enrich community life	satisfy an aesthetic ideal

Eric Routley had it right when he said,

> *We are apt to forget that music in church is not necessarily a unifying influence, a function of friendship, but rather a divisive influence, a generator of resentment. Experience confirms it. Whenever music in a Christian community goes beyond a certain quite elementary degree of sophistication, a division appears between the 'highbrows' and the 'lowbrows', between the professional and the amateur, between the organ console and the pew – with the pulpit becoming an uneasy and often unsuccessful mediator. . . It should be one of the marks of the church's special genius that its music can be satisfying both to the musician of fastidious standards and to the non-musical worshipper.*[4]

The average person in the pew is not unmusical, but simply untrained in the technicalities of sophisticated music, and therefore, according to Routley's description, 'non-musical.' If music is indeed the 'war department' of the church, perhaps it is because it is such an accurate barometer. A special genius *is* required to draw together people of disparate backgrounds, training, and tastes. A very special genius indeed: a very particular enabling of the Holy Spirit.

Hopefully, the distinctions set out in the preceding chart will be helpful to us in finding guidelines for the music we use in worship. For example, why does the choir sing a certain anthem? Is it because Parry wrote it and the bishop is sure to be impressed? Is it because the composer is a celebrity? Or does it serve the need of the worshipping community at a certain point in our service? Does it enrich the life of the community? Discrimination is needed as we apply these criteria.

In contrasting fine art to folk art I have at no point wished to underrate fine art, or to consign it to the concert hall *in toto*. There are many ways to integrate fine art within services of worship, but the yardstick always needs to be, 'Does it enrich our life together?' In speaking of participation, it could be concluded, simplistically I believe, that folk art precludes the possibility of a choir, since the emphasis is on the participation of all. Yet a well-chosen solo or choir anthem can be a powerful tool of communication in worship. No, we shall have to dig for the application of these principles as for gold hidden in our field, our very own church, our very own fellowship. It is there, with the help of the Holy Spirit, that we can discover the answers.

6: Pulling Out All the Stops . . . the musicians' pastoral role

Some of life's funniest things seem to happen in churches. Have you noticed? Once, when I had agreed to become choirmistress for an inner-city church, there was a great kerfuffle concerning the visibility of musicians in the Lord's house. The prevailing opinion was that, unlike children, they should be heard and not seen. This presented some unique problems in a church of modern theatrical design, wihout a single right angle, transept, or stone pillar behind which to hide.

The church warden had an idea! A wooden screen could be installed at the end of the choir stalls nearest the organ console, concealing both organist and director from view of the congregation. Then they would not have to endure the (until now hypothetical) gyrations of the director or the organist's page flipping. It seemed the perfect solution.

However, we had neglected to reckon on one very important feature of the church's theatrical design. Indirect lighting was provided by concealed panels of neon tubing which ran along the walls and behind the organ console. During the first service in which the organist and I were well 'screened', the congregation could not see *us* at all. What they could see, however, was much more frightening. Monstrous great shadows were cast on the walls behind us, as our perfectly normal movements of playing and directing were caught by the light and transformed into science-fiction fantasy!

Now I don't know what you do with the musicians

in your church . . . whether you hide them or try to abide them, venerate them or ignore them; but I would like to explore with you an understanding of the role of the church musician, a role which I believe to be an essentially pastoral one. The pastoring, or care, of the flock which is Christ's church involves the whole area of corporate worship. It is there, within the context of worshipping together, that a group of people can fully experience themselves as belonging to one another, as bearing one another's woes, as celebrating one another's joys, as being God's family here on earth. Music has an enormous potential for strengthening the life of the gathered community. But such potential is not recognized apart from wise and sensitive worship leadership. Not every worship-leader is a musician (for example, the ordained minister), but every musician in the church is involved *de facto* in worship leadership at some level.

Roland Walls tells the story of an English vicar who had a rather anguished concern for the state of the music in his church. It seems that they had a wheezy out-of-tune harmonium which was like the kiss of death on any attempt at praise. Finally he had an inspiration! Since the elderly woman who played the harmonium (badly) arrived each Sunday morning at eight-thirty, the vicar took to arriving at eight o'clock with a watering can in hand. He would then proceed to 'water' the harmonium, and when the organist arrived half an hour later, the keys would be sticking and the instrument quite unplayable!!! Now, it is apparent to me that this vicar, whatever one might think of his tactics, did have his priorities right; he knew that no music at all is better than music which is inappropriate, poorly performed and death-dealing. So he decided to deal a death-blow to the harmonium!

The first requirement for the pastoral musician is

to have a deep personal commitment to praise. I know of no better place to see this than in the life of Job, a man to whom many severe things happened. As you will recall, Job received bad tidings heaped upon bad tidings: first, that his animals had been killed, then his servants; finally his very own children were killed when a house fell on them. How did he receive this news? 'At this,' the story goes, 'Job got up and tore his robe and shaved his head. Then he fell to the ground in worship and said: "Naked I came from my mother's womb, and naked I shall depart. The Lord gave and the Lord has taken away: may the name of the Lord be praised." In all this, Job did not sin by charging God with wrongdoing' (Job 1:20–22).

A dramatic and soul-rending experience is here described tersely. This man, who had suffered so much calamity in his own personal life, poured out his anguish of soul and grief before the Lord. He tore his robes, an action requiring great strength; every muscle, every sinew was involved in this expression of his anguish: then . . . what? Almost in the same breath, as it were, he fell to the ground and worshipped the God who had allowed these great calamities. These two things: the rending of his robe and the falling down to worship, speak to me of the fact that for Job this matter of praising God was no easy thing. He constantly had to bring before God his deepest feelings; he did not hide them. Yet he did not fail to acknowledge God, even in that terrible circumstance. 'May the name of the Lord be praised,' he said. True praise springs from the depths of us, each one of us. It does not happen because we feel happy-clappy. We *may* feel that way. Or, we may feel like tearing our garments. However we feel, God is there. He is in every situation with us. If we can acknowledge him consistently, then we become praising people, people who sense God's presence in a consistent way throughout life.

This commitment to praise has a corporate aspect as well. Some years ago on a university campus in the state of Michigan, U.S.A., there was a notable grass-roots movement in the Roman Catholic Church. As part of a student apostolate on the University of Michigan campus, a young man named Jim Cavnar and several of his friends began to gather, guitars in hand, to sing and praise God in the midst of that secular campus. It was a very simple time of prayer and praise, a happening inspired by the Spirit of God, not a committee decision, not the launching of a new church 'programme'. Because they had a genuine burden to see God's praises set forth in that university community, something happened. (Something will always happen when we have a genuine burden to see God praised). At first there was just a handful of them – only Jim and his friends – but then others began to join them, in tens and twenties, in hundreds and eventually thousands. 'Where two or more are gathered to honour me, true worship will happen.' This is to paraphrase Jesus' words about gathering in his name. Worship will happen for those gathered for that purpose, and it will be available in others, those who might just drop by out of curiosity.

We are called, each of us individually, and all of us together, to a compelling personal encounter with the God whose very being warrants nothing less than our adoration, our praise of him, our awe and wonder. That is the first requirement for the pastoral musician: to seek this encounter. The second thing to seek is an attitude of servanthood. Nowhere is this set forth more graphically than in the second chapter of Paul's epistle to the Philippians:

Your attitude should be the same as that of Christ Jesus: who, being in very nature God, did not consider equality with God something to be grasped, but made himself nothing, taking the very nature of a servant, being made in human likeness. And being found in appearance as a man, he humbled himself and became obedient to death – even death on a cross! Therefore God exalted him to the highest place and gave him the name that is above every name, that at the name of Jesus every knee should bow, in heaven and on earth and under the earth and every tongue confess that Jesus Christ is Lord, to the glory of God the Father (Phil. 2:5–11).

In this definitive passage about servanthood there are three Greek words used to describe the Lord. *Schema* is the word used in the English phrase, 'Being found in appearance (as a man)', and it refers to Jesus' being recognizable as a man, looking like a man, having the outward form of a man. Then there is *gignesthai*, the Greek word which translates 'being made in (human likeness)', a word that tells us something further about the person of Jesus Christ: he was not God-taking-on-the-appearance-of humankind, not God walking around in a man-suit; he was completely and in every respect a man. Both the foregoing words have a connotation of impermanence in the Greek, but the third word *morphe* refers to Jesus' innate, unchangeable, unalterable quality; it is used twice in the passage, once to describe his 'being in *very nature* God', and once to describe his taking 'the *very nature* of a servant'. It is easy to stop short of grasping this, I believe. The incarnational discovery is, for most of us, a life-changing experience, i.e. to know that Jesus really felt the things we feel, was tempted to discouragement, frustration, anger; that he became very tired and hungry – that he was completely human. In our gratitude for this, his so complete identification with our human nature, do we sometimes fail to see the point of it all? Jesus did not *just* take on our humanity; he showed us the essence of it, in being an obedient and willing servant to his Father God. This, he said to us through the manner of life he lived, is what it means to be fully human, fully alive: to be a servant! This is the culmination of our humanity, its finest flowering. When God wanted to reveal the divine nature to us most clearly, God sent a servant-man, Jesus Christ.

Once, when Jesus and his disciples were travelling through Galilee, he began to tell them how he would be delivered into the hands of those who would kill him, and that he would rise again in three days' time. They did not understand what he was telling them, at least not with their rational minds.

Journeying on towards Capernaum, they soon arrived at the house where they were to stay. Jesus asked them, 'What were you arguing about on the road?' (Mark 9:33). Being the good pastor that he was, he was equipped with very sound antennae! There was a prolonged silence; they were ashamed, really, for on the way they had been discussing among themselves which of them was the greatest! (One might pause to consider whether some of our leadership squabbles in the church stem from this same competitive dilemma.)

Jesus dealt with the situation, first of all, by sitting down. The journey had been tiring enough, now this! (I can feel him relax his body weight and emit a sigh as he sits down. He is probably thinking, 'Father, what are we going to do with this lot?') He beckoned them to come sit down too, because he perceived that this was no small matter.

'Are you ready for this, guys?. . . There's something I need to tell you, and it's very different from anything you've grown up with, from any way you have thought in the past. I reckon it's likely to blow your sandals right off your feet.'

Then he said, 'Listen carefully: if anyone would be first, that person must be last of all and the servant of all.'

To become the servant of all is a tremendous statement of vulnerability. It is relatively easy to serve someone whom you love, who is very affirming of you. But *all*, to be the servant of all? Of those who rip us off, who repay our kindnesses with all kinds of ingratitude, or those who do not appear to appreciate us? To serve *them*? In the same passage which we consulted earlier, Paul says to the Philippians, 'Each of you should look not only to your own interests, but also to the interests of others' (Phil. 2:4). Sometimes this seems like a very tall order within the household of faith, not to mention beyond it.

We would do well to ask ourselves whether in fact this calling to servanthood is of the essence of our call to ministry. Or have we fallen in with one of the church's special-interest groups? Do we have a special axe to grind . . . a special cause? Are we really willing to be servants of all? I know some choir-directors who seem prepared to work very hard to make a good 'showing' of their adult choir on Sunday mornings. But as for using music to engage the youth . . . to nurture the children? Sometimes this is not very rewarding, you know. Teenagers are not likely to be your most affirming group while they are groping their way into adulthood. And the care of small children can be very labour-intensive! Yet, if we are called to be the servants of all (not just the adult population) in the church, using music as a communication tool, then the interests of the young children must be seen to be equally as valid as those of adults; and the same applies to youth. A friend of mine from America commented recently on her surprise at the preponderance of elderly and middle-aged people in the churches she had visited in Britain. I wonder how many of the churches she visited use music which their children can tap their feet to, or instruments which young people could learn to play.

What if the professional musician in your church does not have all the gifts necessary to relate to the youth or nurture the children? After all, musicians cannot be expected to be super-people, just as ordained clergy cannot be expected to be equally gifted as pastors, preachers, administrators and spiritual directors. What do we do with our limitations? If a person is a pastoral musician and understands his/her role of servanthood in the Body of Christ, personal shortcomings will not prove a hindrance. Instead, ways will be found to search out, then to encourage and draw out, the needed people with gifts to strengthen the community. These gifts will need activating; these people will need encouraging. And it is within the context of community-building and pastoral health that it can begin to happen.

Today's church musician needs to be an improvisational artist in the broadest sense: bringing together resources of personnel, vocal and instrumental abilities, various age groups, as so many well-tuned stops in a fantasia of praise that truly belongs and is an expression of these very people assembled for worship. I would go one step further; I would say that many church musicians today are improvising with one rank of pipes only; that before the fantasia of praise can pour forth, they must discover the lost ranks, the stops they have never explored, and activate them.

Two of these neglected ranks, I believe, are our youth (teenagers) and our children. As long as we consider them as appendages to the 'real' worship life in our church, we shall be impoverished. This fact came home to me recently when I was asked o sit in on a youth-group meeting; the group had been asked to plan an entire Sunday service – *the* Sunday service for their large and 'renewed' (by which here I mean free to experiment) parish. There was certainly no scarcity of ideas among them! My task, as a sort of liturgical consultant, was to help corral these ideas, giving guidelines without 'taking over', coming alongside them in support of their vision for the service: a challenging assignment! My chief task was to help them comprehend that what they were doing was a gift to God's worshipping family in that place. We talked about timing: the fact that there is drama in good liturgy, that things need to flow with reasonable ease. This led us to some very practical decisions: the group of youth who were to lead the Gradual psalm following the reading of the Old Testament lesson needed to be seated (not necessarily in a formal block) near the front of the church, so that they could take their places easily, say within fifteen seconds. None of them had considered this, but once they got the picture that in the absence of the usual adult choir leadership, people could wonder, 'Well, what's supposed to happen next?', the continuity between the lesson just read and the song to follow would be lost.

The particular song in question was a musical setting of the Psalm for the day which the youth-group leader knew (or thought he knew), but alas! When the time came to practice it, the song was not to be found: not on paper, not in the air, not in the youth leader's fuzzy memory. He tried several times to get it going, using his guitar, but it eluded him (and consequently everyone else.)

'It'll be O.K.,' he assured us in a cool casual manner, 'I'll get it together before Sunday.'

I wasn't at all happy with this, and ventured the notion that we would all feel uncomfortable, not least of all the congregation, if we were unsure of what we were doing come Sunday. The youth leader kept insisting that it had just slipped his mind for the moment, but it was 'no problem, no problem.' Since he was the leader of the group and I was an invited guest at the meeting, it was slightly awkward, and the young people could feel my hesitation, I'm sure. Suddenly one of them spoke up brightly. She said, 'I know . . . I know what we can sing! You know that simple round – it's the very same Psalm!' She began to hum the tune over, and there were affirming nods, 'and,' she added, 'everybody knows it' (more affirming nods). And so it was. Her idea saved the day, and I was struck with the sensitivity of these young people, given a bit of responsibility in the 'real' worship life of their church, and some low-key guidance.

I might add that the cue-sheet which I typed for them, giving practical details like the keys of songs, length of introduction we decided on, who was playing them, etc., was two-thirds of a page in length! They were, after all, not in the same mind-set as a choir which meets week after week to prepare for a Sunday service. They needed just that extra bit of behind-the-scenes preparation and handy reminders so that they could relax and really enjoy carrying off what they had planned. The response of the congregation was tremendously affirmative. People leaving the service were heard to say, 'Why can't we do this once a month?'

Another forgotten rank in our corporate fantasia of praise is our children, those small people whom we like to send off to do 'childish' things. When the Community of Celebration was resident in Yeldall Manor, in Berkshire, England, we held an open meeting once a week in the evening. It was a time of praise and prayer and Bible teaching. Often there would be over one hundred people filling the two large common rooms which conveniently had a folding partition between them. We had quite a number of small children in the community at that time, and the youngest Pulkingham, five-year-old David, was among them. The youngsters used to come to the meeting all dressed for bed, stay for half an hour of praise in song, then march off to bed while we got on with the more 'serious' part of the evening. One morning following the meeting on the night before, David said to me,

'Why do you always save the good songs 'til the children have gone to bed?'

I was floored. We had been singing lots of happy, rhythmic songs (including some action songs like the 'Butterfly Song', and all of them planned with the children's presence in mind.)

'What do you mean by *good* songs, David?' I asked.

Cocking his blonde head to one side, he thought for a moment, then rattled off a string of them:

'Alleluia! Sing to Jesus' (we always sang it to 'Hyfrydol'), 'The Bread of Life', 'Alleluia Number One' . . . the list went on, and suddenly I caught the import of what he was saying. These were the deep, worshipful songs which, within the context of a prayer and praise meeting, tended to happen when the people were caught up in a strong sense of God's presence. So, inadvertantly, we were offering the children an appetizer and sending them off without any meat and potatoes . . . *and they knew it* (that's what astounded me.) I have never, since that very moment, underestimated the ability of a child to be involved in worship – providing, of course, that the adults are themselves able to be lifted out of themselves into God's exalted praises.

Servanthood with respect to children may take the form of listening to what their hearts are saying, then finding a way to respond; with young people it may take the form of making space for their exercise of responsibility, and supporting them behind the scenes. The demands of servanthood will come along different lines depending on the age-group and the circumstances, but the essence is the same: making ourselves vulnerable and ready to serve *all*. This leads us quite naturally into what I believe to be the third thing needful for the pastoral musician: a gift for creating family.

The 'family' we are helping to create in the church is one where all the members receive the same care and concern. Have you ever noticed how easy it is for parents to love the affable, lovable child, and how very difficult to love the diffident, the obstinate, the rebellious? It would seem that the child who received the good' genes and displays the winsome parental characteristics gets lots of favourable attention. The one who displays the least likeable genes is much harder to love! So, in our family which is the church, we have our problem children too, do we not? Perhaps yours is a very traditional church, and God has sent you a 'charismaniac' who, at the drop of a hat, flings his arms skyward, all but knocking hymnals out of the hands of the person next to him! Or perhaps yours is a church which has happily embraced the new liturgies, and on the back row of the church God has stationed a faithful but obstinate soul who insists on saying the old form of the Lord's Prayer *largo*, *fortissimo*, while everyone else is saying the new form *andante cantabile*. Perhaps these are some of our problem children. How do we relate to them? Hopefully, we will find a way, remembering that love overcomes a multitude of things – insensitivity, obstinancy and every other form of sin.

Relationships always have a particular 'tone' to them; one can sense it. Parental relationships have an 'I'm up here and you're down there and I will tell you what is best for you' tone. Professional relationships tend to be coloured by a tone of one-upmanship. Hierarchical relationships tend to make the person on the bottom of the heap feel like a nobody (to the extent that some will even find it hard to look their superiors in the eye.) Relationships in the family which is the Church are characterized by mutual care for each other, as members one of another, as peers if you will. Our Western culture offers us fragmentation, for we live in a pluralistic society which caters for every possible age and interest group one could imagine. This is why worship has been called the tireless work of the entire community. It *is* work, there is no doubt about it. And it is a Monday – Saturday work which can cause Sundays to blossom.

The work of creating family in the church is a very costly one; the healing of relationships doesn't just happen. There has to be a constant work of reconciliation going on, in families, between age-groups, between classes, between professional interests, etc. This is the difficult path to the glorious unity of the Trinity; would any of us choose an easier one? For the truth is. . .

> *The Trinity*
>   *is . . . community in unity*
> *and gives community in unity.*
> *There is a whole thornbush of*
>   *desires*
>   *moods*
>   *antipathies*
>   *culture*
>   *habits*
> *to get through before we enter the*
>   *joy of the Trinity –*
>   *community in unity.*
> *We can't just walk into it as*
>   *we would walk into a cinema!*
> *Reconciliation is a costly thing;*
> *It has to do with taking pain into*
>   *ourselves, enduring it.*

*We don't just put up with one another;
we endure the pain of one another's
weaknesses.**

Shall we receive this glorious gift, community in unity, with all its pain and challenge, and its joys too?

* from the unpublished works of Roland Walls and used with his kind permission.

81

7: Follow the Leader . . . folk leadership in worship

> *Remember that music we turned our backs on a few years ago? It did not die out as we had imagined or hoped, but is alive and well and evolving nicely in the Catholic Church, where it has been absorbed into the fabric of worship.*[1]

Maureen M. Morgan, writing candidly to her colleagues in the American Guild of Organists, draws attention to the phenomenon of the late sixties and early seventies: a new surge of folk music (or people's music) in the church.

What is it that makes this music so appealing? Perhaps we should examine one song in detail to find specific answers:

Allelu   Mimi Farra

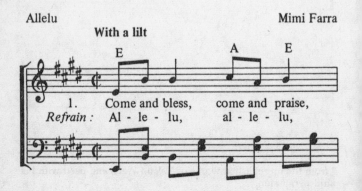

come and__ praise the liv - ing God.
al - le - lu - ia, Je - sus Christ.

Al-le-lu, al - le-lu, al-le - lu - ia, Je-sus

final ending

Christ._____

2. Come and seek, come and find,
~~Come and find the living God.~~
Allelu, allelu,
Alleluia, Jesus Christ. *Refrain.*

3. Come and hear, come and know,
Come and know the living God.
Allelu, allelu,
Alleluia, Jesus Christ. *Refrain.*

4. Come and bless, come and praise,
Come and praise the Word of
God;
Word of God, Word made flesh,
Alleluia, Jesus Christ. *Refrain.*

83

Note the amount of repetition built into the song. The verse, sung by the folk leader, lines out the melody which the people will sing on the refrain. When the time comes for them to sing 'Allelu', the melody is already in their heads; it practically sings itself! Yet they are not just parroting the folk leader, because the verse extends an invitation ('Come and bless, come and praise') to which they and they alone have the response 'Allelu'. This structure works like magic: it gives people the feeling that they are creating, in their dialogue with the folk leader, a fresh vehicle of praise. The song proves very contagious; it is almost impossible not to sing!

The form of the music is reminiscent of that used by our Jewish forebears. A hallmark of synagogue worship was the *Cantus Responsorious*, a twofold method of singing shared between soloist and people (the soloist singing a phrase and the people repeating it, or answering it with a refrain.) In use from ancient times, the *Cantus Responsorius* was '. . . clearly the natural result of having present at the service both skilled and unskilled singers.'[2]

The happy blend of skilled and unskilled seems to be one of the keys to the appeal of folk music. Think for a moment about the anthem as an art form. Because it presumes a skilled performing group, a choir, its rendition, whether good or bad, seems to focus attention on quality. 'Wasn't the choir magnificent this morning?!' reflects a good performance. 'Whatever did happen to the tenors in the *'Ave Verum'* . . . were they in the wrong key?' is a different sort of post-mortem. But in either case the attention seems inescapably focused on quality. The hymn, on the other hand, is a form which can be rousingly-to-reluctantly sung without eliciting comment, because a hymn is a hymn is a hymn. It is not expected to win accolades aesthetically since it is a vehicle for the unskilled to sing. It may prove a very satisfying vehicle; or at times, because little is ventured, little will be gained in the singing. Into this gap – between the quality-consciousness of the anthem and the dull-normal expectation of the hymn – comes the responsorial folk song, a blending of skilled and unskilled which creates a new dimension, a dialogue. The synthesis allows the people (unskilled) to participate in the creation of something beautiful and takes the focus off the 'performer' (soloist) by having the latter rub elbows, so to speak, with the ordinary folk. The expert and inexpert are no longer polarized; they have met somewhere in the middle and are free to enjoy one another's company!

Accessibility or ease of participation is certainly another key to the appeal of folk music. A gifted folk leader gives as much rhythmic direction to the music as the symphony conductor with baton in hand! One notable difference between the two is that the strumming arm of the guitarist (clearly visible to the people) is an organic part of the music-making rather than an added tool to help keep things together. The well-schooled folk leader uses the mouth to mirror words of songs; even without benefit of a wordsheet people can be drawn into the music, taking the words, as it were, right out of the folk leader's mouth! It's as simple as that. The musical sophisticate may call it spoon-feeding, but whatever it is called, it is in fact a very effective way to facilitate the learning of new music. In the musical example we saw earlier ('Allelu') neither a music book or wordsheet would be necessary in order to teach the song. In fact, they would be counter-productive, because the song's genius is its simple repetitive structure, which makes it ideal for rote-learning.

Folk or 'people's' music is, above all, friendly music. It is welcoming to the total stranger, it embraces a common humanity in its penchant for contagious rhythms and memorable melodies. 'Friendly' is an apt desription for both the structure of this music and its manner of presentation. Unquestionably, it is THE MUSIC for use in Christian worship in the countries of the Third World. Why then, one might ask, is there such controversy over the use of this type of music in the Western world? More accurately, in the Western church, for certainly the 'world' knows how to handle simple music with contagious rhythms! Was Luther (a product of Western culture) right when he protested that the Devil shouldn't have all the good times to himself? Was he reflecting a Western dilemma?

There is no question that, in the Western world, the history of liturgical practice shows a tension between that which is sublime, 'other-worldly', and that which is earthy, close to the marketplace. The former we call, rather blithely I believe, 'sacred'; the latter we call 'secular'. Yet most of us would agree that this is the very barrier which Christ came to break down, destroying through his incarnation the wall that had existed between God and humankind, between the holy and the human. Leo the Great, inspired by God to articulate, on behalf of the whole church, the nature of the God-man, illuminated the Council of Chalcedon in the year 451 A.D. with a definition of the divine and human natures in the person of Christ. These natures, he affirmed, are indivisible. One and the same Christ is acknowledged as '. . . Son, Lord, Only-begotten, recognized in two natures, without confusion, without change, without division, without separation. . .'[3] Perhaps we should not be surprised to find the tension of containing the two natures reflected in the life of the church. Perhaps we would do well to embrace it, seeing in it and through it the genuine effort of the church throughout history to follow its leader.

A brief look at some of the highlights of our Western liturgical history may be helpful. Tracing them is in many ways like following the course of a giant pendulum swinging between that which reflects the highest, the holy, and that which truly touches our humanity. At the end of the sixth century Pope Gregory the Great sent the prior of St Andrews' Monastery in Rome to England. He brought with him thirty-nine companions, including a cantor and highly skilled singers. From that time on, 'England began to absorb into its musical system the principles of the Gregorian monodic chant, and some order was brought to the music of the church.'[4]

Swinging in another direction, the Franciscan order (established in 1224) encouraged the use of popular songs and carols in the towns and villages where people often met at 'preaching crosses' in the open air. There was a free exchange of secular and religious words in their songs. The well-loved macaronic carol grew out of this freedom to 'mix and match', combining a verse in the vernacular with a Latin refrain. Such practices were at times severely condemned by the authorities of the church because they disliked the 'heart of the sacred liturgy being corrupted by the secular.'[5]

So one can observe a counter-trend developing, away from simplicity towards very ornate and highly embellished liturgical music, to the extent that sometimes even the lessons were sung in complex polyphony during the fourteenth and fifteenth centuries. But looming on the horizon was the Reformation with its heavy emphasis on congregational participation in worship. Reformers like Erasmus of Rotterdam bemoaned the state of church music in his day: 'Modern church music,' he said (from his vantage point in the sixteenth century), 'is so constructed that the congregation cannot hear a single word clearly, and the choristers themselves do not understand what they are singing.'* Luther himself, although not opposed to choirs, favoured hearty singing by the congregation (in churches) and by families (in homes.) 'It is my intention,' he said, 'to make German psalms for the people, spiritual songs whereby the Word of God may be kept alive in them by singing . . . I desire that new-fangled and courtly expressions may be avoided and that the words may all be exceedingly simple and common, such as plain folk may understand.'[6] Luther and the other Reformers undoubtedly sensed the community-building properties of music; they were not afraid to admit the use of secular tunes in the divine service.

But some of the Reformers took a different, and very extreme, view. On All Saint's Day in England in 1552, when The Second Book of Common Prayer (heavily influenced by John Knox) was launched in St Paul's Cathedral, 'the choir was dispersed, the organ silenced, and the officiants, according to the directions of the new rubric, wore neither alb, vestment, nor cope. Protestantism was enthroned in all its starkness at the heart of England's religious life.'[7] And so the chronicle continues, we trace the revival of 'church music' in England at the time of the restoration of the monarchy, when the status and function of the choir was reinstated by the pithy Prayer Book rubric, 'in quires and places where they sing, here followeth the anthem.' We watch the birth of modern hymnody as we know it, under the leadership of the Wesley brothers in the eighteenth century. They knew full well that people will remember basic doctrines of their faith if they commit them to

* from his *Commentary to the New Testament*, vol. 2, 1 Cor. 14:19.

memory in song. Another phenomenon of the eighteenth century was the gallery minstrels, *ad hoc* groups of instrumentalists drawn from the local townsfolk, enlivening the worship with their varieties of sounds: flute, cello, bassoon, banjo, concertina! This period, with its vibrant village worship seems to have achieved a real synthesis of sacred and secular styles. But the early nineeenth century witnessed a low ebb in church music, and it is not surprising to learn of another pendulum swing thereafter, an attempt to restore quality to the 'fallen' state of musical standards in the cathedral choral service, and on . . . and on . . . and on. . .

Perhaps there are a few conclusions we can draw from even such a cursory glance at history. Two parallel streams of thought seem to travel right the way through: on the one hand, a great concern for the transcendent beauty of worship, and on the other hand, an equally great concern for how music can reach ordinary people. Is it too much to hope that ours might be the century of integration of these two values within the Christian church? Do we see this as a part of the kingdom coming? Given the fact that cathedral worship will always have a grand scope and the small parish church/mission/congregation will always have limited resources, is there any reason why the latter cannot experience awesome beauty in worship? . . . or the former a friendly sense of ease in participation? Is such integration possible? I believe that it is. There are many who would maintain that the contrast between 'secular' and 'sacred' music is not as absolute as has often been claimed. 'It is extremely difficult, if not impossible, to give an *a priori* definition of sacred and secular style in music, and to determine on this basis in what way the one may have effected the other. The distinction of secular and sacred is essentially one of musical function, not of musical style.'[8]

Yet astute observers of the present age in the church's life, such as Maureen Morgan, point to the fact that increased training for musicians in post-World War II in the United States has led to the development of very rigid ideas as to what constitutes appropriate music for the worship of God. The prevailing style, she says, has been

> . . . *dominantly western European. Any musician who adopted a worship style that fell outside this parameter would be considered not to be an AGO* type. . . The developing inflexibility of this outlook was on a collision course with the explosion of folk music in the church, a direction given a powerful thrust by the peace movement and the concern of a large number of people for human rights. Curiously, those interests were not significant in the church until the secular world forced them into the sacred arena. Musicians were unable to stop this invasion.*[9]

If this analysis is correct, it would certainly not be the first time God had used events outside the church to correct and inform the church. Recalling Peter's vision of the white sheet lowered from heaven, full of hitherto forbidden meats considered unclean by Jewish law, and the Lord's words to him, 'Do not call anything impure that God has made clean' (Acts 10:15), we might ponder whether we in the church have had a tendency to legalize certain styles of music as 'sacred' and summarily dismiss the rest as 'impure'. If so, we would do well to take a second look, particularly since the majority of the Christian world today does *not* in fact adhere to the Western aesthetic models.

* The American Guild of Organists

Let's return to our earlier question, 'What is it that makes folk music so appealing?' The answers suggested were ease of participation, a happy blending of unskilled and skilled into one 'happening', and a quality of friendliness. I would now like to think about the kind of leadership which makes such music possible in our churches. For in my experience many, if not most, trained musicians in the church feel lost or inadequate in dealing with it. It's just not their cup of tea! And this very fact undoubtedly accounts for their reluctance-to-resistance in embracing it. What do we *do* with it, for heaven's sake?

It is for heaven's sake, I believe, that we will struggle to find a way to do something with it. First of all, the trained musician must know his/her own long and short suits. There are some trained musicians who are also good folk musicians, but such is not necessarily the case. The folk musician is primarily an 'out-front' communicator; the trained musician may be a communicator (in terms of personality) or a person whose primary gifts lie behind the scenes as teacher or accompanist or solo instrumentalist. But one thing is for sure: the folk musician, this person with a special ability to draw people together in song, needs access to the disciplined skills of the trained musician. A gift for song and spontaneity and a way with people does not produce – on its own – a liturgical musician.

Ultimately, the burden is on the back of the 'professional' church musician to befriend and come alongside the folk musician in the church. I do not think one needs a syllabus in order to offer friendship and discover ways to work with the folk musician. The problem, really, is to find the appropriate venue. So often we skirt the encounter entirely by organizing our services into choral services (which need the trained organist/choir-director's services) and youth services or 'praise' meetings (where the folk leader and followers can do their thing – be it ever so atrocious in quality.) It amazes me that more trained musicians don't lose sleep over this situation! But in all fairness, there is not infrequently a bit of resistance on the other side as well, a resistance against discipline, practice and the attendant tedium that goes with it. Clearly, we have just stumbled onto a problem that goes far beyond music, or what kind of music, or what sort of musicians. Are we really given to serve one another in our local church? Are we willing to become vulnerable, to reveal our ignorances? Are we willing to be wrong . . . to change a previously held opinion? Is the quality of our fellowship that important to us?

If it is, then we will find a way to offer our gifts which builds up the Body of Christ rather than fragmenting it. Perhaps the first task of music directors is to seek a grounding in fellowship, whatever it may cost, and not to rest content with a 'live and let live' philosophy. Surely if we are one body, sharing one bread – that bread being Christ – then there will be a costly caring for one another in the various ministries of the local church. Music directors would do well to assess their own 'short suits' and to seek those complementary gifts to their own which are resident within the local church. (If they are not resident, then the next task is to pray for the Lord to send them!) The next task is to activate those gifts, by any and all means available. The third thing will be to learn to work alongside those whom the Holy Spirit sends to you, regarding them as co-workers in the kingdom of the Son of love. Ah! this may well be the key to it all: to see through the eyes of love those whom God sends to us (and God *will* send us helpers if we are open and seeking and desiring such.)

What, then, do these two people – the trained

musician and the folk leader – have to offer each other? The folk leader has a natural gift of communication, making it easy for people to learn new music – either by their mirroring what the (visible) leadership is doing, or by the use of simple phrase-by-phrase techniques when needed. This capability addresses a big problem: how to overcome the resistance in many congregations to that which replaces the tried and true! If the learning process can be not only painless but actually enjoyable, then the folk leader will already have served a very good purpose. Short, five-minute congregational rehearsals before a service go down well with this 'troubadour' type of leadership; because the folk leader identifies so completely with the 'folk', the latter are not likely to feel they are being forced to be choristers. The folk leader is able to be a clown when needed, and to activate that sense of play which makes us all more truly human. As George MacDonald aptly reminds us, 'It is the heart that is not yet sure of its God that is afraid to laugh in His presence.' Yet another advantage of folk leadership is the portability of its musical instruments. It is easy to take a guitar or hand drum to a picnic, or a house meeting, and the use of the same instruments – and hopefully some of the same songs – in the Sunday liturgy makes for a strengthening of the community through its music. (Well, it's true, isn't it? Which of us has ever seen a pipe organ at a picnic?)

The professional musician, in turn, has much to offer the folk leader. In the first place, sound musicianship; a sure-footed knowledge of the elements of music, of rhythm, melody and harmony, as well as musical form, which make it possible to step into a new idiom with basic guidelines intact. This means that you may offer suggestions based on your musical experience and ear-training, taking into account the idiomatic nature of the instruments you are dealing with. Folk music derives its charm from a marriage of melody and rhythm against a very simple harmonic background (the natural parameters of a strummed instrument.) The organ, on the other hand, derives most of its magic from a kaleidoscope of harmonic colours, constantly changing: from dark to bright, rich to dissonant. It likes to do 'creepy' things; not so the guitar. As our look at 'Stille Nacht' showed, a one-per-bar chord change was more than enough! The organ can, however, play in concert with the guitar because of its orchestral scope: it may use a solo flute or reed to play a melody against a strummed (guitar) background, or it may provide a string backing to sustain harmonies while the guitar gives a rhythmic thrust to the music. These are just two of many possibilities. Bach would likely have rejoiced at the combination of organ with guitar, as the two are remarkably compatible!

What is the meeting place, in terms of repertoire, for two such contrasting instruments as the organ and the guitar? The traditional hymnal sitting in nearly every church pew-rack will provide an ample place to meet. There we will find numerous tunes like 'Stille Nacht' whose simple folk origins make them 'naturals' for the wedding of the two. Examples which spring immediately to mind are tunes like 'St Columba', 'Kingsfold', and 'Land of Rest.' Here 'Kingsfold' is arranged with flowing piano accompaniment, guitar chords, and an obligato for flute (see over).

It is thoroughly possible to integrate the folk origins of such songs with their later development as four-part hymns – within the same arrangement. For example, one might alternate unison stanzas accompanied by guitar and stanzas with four-part vocal harmonies as printed in traditional hymnals. Melding the traditional 'church' sound of the organ with folk instrumentation helps to integrate agegroups,

'Kingsfold'
Traditional English melody
Arr. Betty Pulkingham

Horatius Bonar

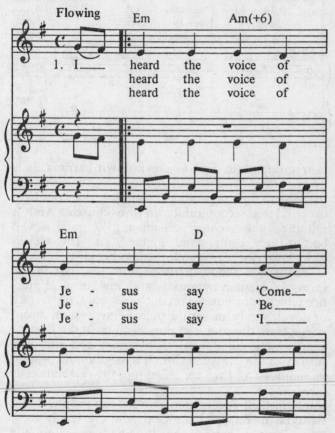

1. I heard the voice of
   heard the voice of
   heard the voice of

Je - sus say 'Come
Je - sus say 'Be
Je - sus say 'I

(cont.)

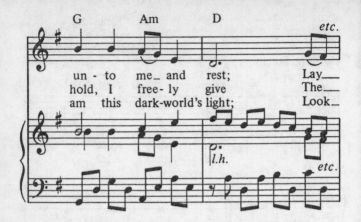

taste-groups, etc. and to break down barriers. It is fragmenting and short-sighted, I believe, to perpetuate their separation; it certainly does not help to build true community in the church. And it reinforces the 'we/they' dilemma: ('We go at eleven because we can't stand guitars', or 'The eleven o'clock service seems so formal and cold.')

We have a goodly heritage from the past in the form of Christian hymnody, and any liturgical practice which concentrates on the 'now' only, the trendy or novel, surely misses the point. The present, disengaged from the past, can provide at most the fleeting beauty of a cut flower, then wither and die. The history of the Christian church is its glory, its beauty, its richness; and we are called into the celebration as late-comers, to join the angels, the archangels, the saints in their several generations, the prophets and martyrs, to proclaim the God who created history, then limited himself to it. Shall we join the celebration? Shall we take a deep breath and let the Lord enlarge our vistas, challenge our presuppositions? For some of us this may mean abandoning our prejudice against using guitars in church; for some it may mean allowing ourselves to fall in love with our heritage of hymnody. But whatever it means, we will all most surely be challenged to come up into a larger place where we can see a broader view of God's activity than we may have done in the past.

8: Choirs Ancient and Modern . . . which is yours?

Oh, the rising of the sun
and the running of the deer,
The playing of the merry organ,
sweet singing in the choir.[1]

Reading these lines, you can almost hear the tolling bells of the village church beckoning to all within earshot. Closing your eyes, you can glimpse the steeple punctuating the village skyline, all the cottages huddling close to one another for comfort in the cold winter months. As the smoke circles upwards from each chimney, so the strains of 'Forest Green' ascend, warming the crisp night air. A lovely sight? A familiar and well-loved sound?

It makes one stop to ponder our situation today. Few of us live in 'Christmas card' villages, and the tempo of urban life makes the scene above seem fanciful and far away. Quaint! And yet, if we were pressed to analyse our responses, most of us would discover a place of yearning within us for the simple celebration of life in the village community. A place where one is almost certain to be known, and is likely to be known – warts and all – very well indeed. Many visionaries today are heralding an age in which the church will best be seen in microcosm – little groups formed and nurtured by the Spirit of God, living out the life of the Son of God's love in local community after local community. The church of the future may well hoist the banner of 'Small is Beautiful', and in the meantime?

The church is grappling with the depersonalisation of our increasingly technological society, and trying to find ways to supply meaning and a sense of belonging for today's urban mobilites. The mega-church offers yet one more place to be anonymous, a face in the crowd, so it really does not fill the deepest needs of people today. And if we tend to think that huge choirs and elaborate ceremonial somehow impress people and make them think that God is a great and splendid being, we may need to think again.

> *If this was ever so, it is not so now. People are not impressed by a splendid ceremonial performed by people whose lives do not reflect what their worship expresses. It is seen nowadays (though St Benedict said it long ago) that glory can be given to God only through the lives* of those who worship him.[2]

The thrust of contemporary liturgy, including its helpmate, church architecture, is towards belonging-ness, involvement and ease of participation. Where does the church choir fit into this picture? Is it an outmoded institution in today's participatory liturgies? There is every indication that the sentiments of the chorister who sang,*

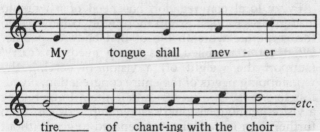

My tongue shall nev-er tire of chant-ing with the choir *etc.*

* ('When Morning Guilds the Skies', verse 3, translation by E. Caswell, 1868; music by J. Bornby.)

are not shared by many of today's churchgoers. In many places choirs have been abandoned altogether. In others, newly-spawned folk groups are not only leading the music at services, but also involving in active outreach through music – to hospitals, ecumenical gatherings, etc. attracting an increasing membership of singers and instrumentalists; while the traditional choir in the same church languishes for want of new members or new vision! In other situations a strong reactionary leadership of the choir has served to throttle new, creative expressions of a congregation's life. Perhaps contemporary choirs need to re-define their roles if they are to serve the church in a vital way.

> *Why do we automatically assume that if there is no choir, it follows that there is no music? Why should music in worship apparently hinge so much on the presence of a choir, however small or large a part they play in any worship situation? If there is no choir, and whatever the reason for this, it follows that the hymns and any other vocal music will of necessity have to be sung by the congregation. For many of us, this will be a new concept and a new responsibility for which we must adapt ourselves.*[3]

Every local congregation has need of a worship leadership group, a group thoroughly committed to the corporate worship life of that body of people. Whatever it is called, this group needs to 'carry' (support the weight of) a vision of serving the worshipping needs of the entire congregation. Needless to say, such a group cannot attain to or realize a vision without visionary leadership, nor can it go further than its leaders are prepared to go. Without a vision to inspire activity and impel onward movement, the people truly perish, as the writer of Proverbs reminds us. Many choirs today are lacking in such visionary leadership, I believe. Many less formalized and tradition-orientated groups are flourishing because they *do* have a strong sense of vision and purpose, despite, in some cases, a lack of expertise and training.

You will note that, to this point, I have said little about music. That is because I believe music is a secondary concern for the worship leadership group in the church. While this notion may cause great gnashing of teeth in some quarters, I feel it needs to be said. Music itself, that wonderful tool of communication which can draw together and focus an entire group of people, be they fifty or five thousand, is in danger of becoming a prey to factions within the church. Once we can establish the vision of a servant-body within the church whose purpose is to aid *all* of God's assembled people to be released into praise, then we can talk about music, the means. This will rule out the possibility of turning the church choir into a choral society. (Why not form a choral society for its own sake?) It will also prevent groups whose chief desire is to entertain and do music for fun, or groups like the one described above who have an excited sense of ministry through music, from drawing membership away from the 'traditional' choir and setting up divisions within the church. Many churches are big enough in membership and broad enough in ministry scope to support several choirs, folk groups, etc. But it is important, I believe, to have *one visible* group who are clearly responsible for and committed to the *entire* worship life of that particular family of God. Call it a choir if you are comfortable with that word and it feels expandable to you. Call it the music group, or the music ministry, but whatever else you do, put all of the eggs of worship concern into one basket for 'someones' to carry! They will then serve as a microcosm of the worshipping family-of-God in that place, a living symbol of bringing all of our lives before God in praise. They will provide the spiritual backbone of the music ministry in that place, a strong pastoral help to the ordained and trained ministry. How does one impart such a vision? By catching it first oneself! Since the 'vision' is the content and burden of this book, I will not be-labour it here.

What, then, are some of the practical ways that the church choir can serve the whole congregation? Certainly, the most basic function of such a group is to undergird congregational singing. A friend of mine, a choir-master in Berkshire, had a strong reaction from his choir when he asked them to sing some hymns in unison. Apparently, they had the idea that 'choir' equals sopranos, altos, tenors and basses, full-stop! Yet strong unison singing is unparalleled in its unifying, focusing quality. And frequently a new hymn may need to be sung for a time in unison before the people are secure enough that the choir can 'leave' them and sing parts. If a choir is unappreciative of the beauty of unison singing, learning a special anthem which depends for its effect on sensitive unison sound may help to win them over! Or it is possible to find material within the content of hymnody which will serve the same purpose. Calvin Hampton's 'The Church's One Foundation' has an ethereal beauty when sung by well-blended women's voices,

1. The Church's one ___ foun-da - tion ___

___ Is Je - sus Christ her ___ Lord;

Herbert Howell's 'All My Hope on God is Founded' has a sturdy quality which is gratifying for male voices (see over). Have the women sing a unison stanza for the men, and the men for the women, remembering that ninety per cent of good singing is good listening, i.e. hearing something of beauty which you can emulate. The voices of men and women have a natural complementary quality which is God-given, so do not fail to make use of the contrasts they afford.

How can hymn-singing be exciting? Quite simply,

Unison

All my hope on God is found - ed;

he doth still my trust re - new ...

I believe, by our getting inside each hymn we sing, exploring its word-content and meaning, catching the spirit of the music to which it is set, and varying our treatment of it according to its demands. Knowing how a particular hymn fits into the overall shape of a service is helpful. Sometimes, knowing how a hymn came to be written builds appreciation, and there are numerous books available which chronicle the stories of hymns and their writers. Added to this is the opportunity most directors have of actually meeting, or having indirect contact (through recordings, journals, etc.) with contemporary hymn-writers and performing groups. This will enable them to present hymnody to the choir not as a corpus of music by dead people (!) but as a living, growing tradition to which there are exciting contemporary chapters to be added.

For example, it is interesting to learn about the little song 'Neighbours' which has proven so useful in contemporary worship. It came to us through the ministry of Tom Colvin. While serving as a missionary to Ghana he collected much indigenous African music and made it available in a little booklet* published by the Iona Community (of which he is a member). This pursuit could easily lead to by-roads of enrichment, e.g. learning more about the work of the Iona Community and the history of Iona itself, hearkening to the island's rich Celtic heritage and to St Columba. Perhaps before long we might find occasion to sing the beautiful Irish melody 'St Columba' (associated with the paraphrase of Psalm 23, 'The King of Love My Shepherd is'). There are no end of ways to experience the richness of our history through the hymns we sing.

One thing is certain: a congregation of very ordinary people can be ignited to hymn-singing provided the flame has been lit in the leadership first! Is the hymn a bold proclamation? Is it gentle and lyrical? Is it rhythmic and bright? The leadership must *know* what it is and communicate this through the sounds that are made. Have you ever attended a service where the hymns all sounded exactly alike? Or have you attended over a period of time and noticed that a particular hymn seemed *always* to be sung at a set tempo and in a well-rutted, habitual way (almost as

* 'Free to Serve' (Hymns from Africa), Iona Community Pub. Dept., Glasgow.

though it had been set on 'automatic pilot')? As I read the Psalms I am impressed with the fact that God never once directs us to sing 'old' songs, but only new ones!

The Spirit of God is a creative, ever-moving spirit, infusing new life into everything we touch. As we pick up our hymnals to sing, we are preparing for the Spirit of God to re-create this piece of music – through us. It is significant that the Spirit is characterized by *breath*, as is also our singing. When we sing, we are acutely aware of breathing (much more so than in ordinary activities.) We sing musical phrases, punctuated by breathing places. We breathe as we sing; the Spirit of God breathes new life into old hymns as we sing them. They become new songs, even though they are old. The breath of the Spirit re-creates them through us – living, breathing, Spirit-empowered beings.

New liturgies in today's church have given birth to mountains of new music, and the choir can perform heroics in helping a congregation learn it! One of the charms of folk music is its propensity for refrain-and-verse form; the choir can take responsibility for learning verses to many such songs, leaving the people with only the easily remembered refrain to sing. In some cases, the verses of a song may be 'congregational', i.e. straightforward enough to be easily learned by people, given time and repetition. In this case, the choir's singing of the verses will be part of a strategy: they will do so until the congregation absorbs the verses and becomes comfortably familiar with them.

In other cases we may choose to have a soloist or the choir sing the verses of a song – not *until* the people catch on, but because they never will! Some verses are exceptionally wordy for congregational singing, or have rhythmic subtleties of the sort which tend to trip people up. A good example is the ballad.

Lord of the Dance by Sydney Carter has verses which tell a story and a refrain which offers a response. The verses are clearly too irregular to be good congregational material; the refrain is bright and easy to remember. Well sung verses will inspire the congregation to sing their part, the refrain, well; and the result will be a satisfying experience. The congregation will have added a new title to their repertoire in a rather painless fashion! As a choir demonstrates its flexibility and willingness to try new things, the people can be led into them in a spirit of adventure – provided, of course, that the new has not been allowed to sweep away the old, but has rather been integrated with it.

Flexibility, then, is a needed gift which the music leadership can provide for the people. The 'people' come in many shapes and sizes representing such varied backgrounds, that it is small wonder the leadership needs flexibility in order to serve their needs. It may be helpful to look at some of the more frequently encountered needs in today's church.

More and more urban congregations are being challenged to move across ethnic barriers, creating friendship. Bi-lingual celebrations, headsets tuned into a translation of the sermon for an ethnic minority group, sign-language: all of these bespeak a complex urban society struggling to 'come as one' before the Lord. Spanish, the language of eighty per cent of the neighbourhood, became so central to the life and ministry of the Church of the Redeemer in Houston, Texas, that the choir, predominantly Anglo-Americans, learned to sing in Spanish! They spent many hours at disciplined drills in pronunciation and singing, in order that they might sing in Spanish with no less excellence than their best efforts in their own native tongue. Their concern as choir echoed the concern of the entire church for the changing neighbourhood in which it found itself, a concern implemented in many neighbourhood ministries: e.g. teaching English to non-English speaking members of the community, teaching Spanish to many of the Anglo-Americans in the congregation, running a thrift shop for neighbourhood residents, etc. The music sung on Sunday mornings was in this case the tip of the iceberg. The choir served to reflect, through music, the life of the congregation as they came before the Lord in the midst of the teeming life of the inner city.

Serving the needs of the youth within the church also requires flexibility. This may sound like the understatement of the year, and many will opt for the easier path of letting the youth do their own thing. But for those with ears to hear and eyes to see, it will be possible to follow the youth's lead at times and do 'their thing' with them. I recall a particular Advent season when the liturgy group at the Church of the Redeemer put together an Advent songsheet for use in family worship. It contained one song, 'My Lord, he is 'a-comin' soon' which had a catchy, rhythmic refrain and soul-music sound.

way   of   the   Lord._____

('My Lord, he is a-comin' soon' by
Laura Winnen & Jeff Cothran)

A gifted folk leader introduced it to the pre-teens group during the Sunday school hour. The 'hook' (that irresistable something that reaches out and grabs you) was finger-snapping. The folk leader established the rhythmic beat in her own mind, then started snapping her fingers on the off-beat; the children followed suit, and when the rhythmic pattern was firmly established and everyone was involved, she simply sang the refrain to the accompaniment of the finger snaps. That was her teaching method, a perfect example of that which is caught rather than taught! The song captured the youths' fancy, and by the end of Advent had become 'top of the pops'. It eventually found its way into a Sunday liturgy, at which point the choir simply got on board with something that had originated with the younger members of the church and worked its way up (?). Not really up, but out and around, permeating the whole. What a pity if all the songs of this contagious, involving sort, are kept only for the Sunday school hour and 'for the kids.' The adults will be the impoverished ones!

The case-study of the song above shows how things happen in a living, moving, evolving church structure. The planning mechanisms were subject to fellowship, that access to one another which allows changes to be made and corporate decisions taken. No one had the slightest inkling that this little song would catch on as it did; but when it happened, there was provision within the congregation's life to

109

respond to the reality. This sort of sensitive involvement with youth, variously known as 'picking up the vibes' or 'going with the flow,' is surely one of the best gifts we can give them.

With younger children, consistency and a well-laid plan will be our strongest card. Thoughtful planning on the part of the music director and Sunday school teachers may open up opportunities to incorporate the children's simple offering of song into our services. The inter-generational make up of the Body of Christ will keep us on our toes in our local setting, if we really *do* look '. . . not only on our own concerns but on those of others' (Phil. 2:4). We shall be concerned with the very young, as well as with the elderly. And we shall be concerned with the dying.

The choir can provide a pastoral presence at a funeral which does more than talk about Christ's victory over death. Proclaiming this truth through music is a powerful ministry to the bereaved. Once again I turn to the Church of the Redeemer, Houston, Texas, as at least one choir that I know of which has, year in and year out over the past twenty years, served the needs of the families in the congregation by being present at funerals. Obviously, not all members could be present for all funerals, since by their nature they do not fall into predictable time slots, but the representation of the choir has been vigorous, often at great personal inconvenience to individual members: a servant body.

Weddings, services of baptism, and many other special occasions in the church's ongoing life call forth an opportunity for service from the choir. And, within the parameters which the ordained minister and music director supply, great flexibility will be required here also. A wedding, for example, while adhering to very strict ecclesiastical guidelines (which would prevent the use of music for purely sentimental reasons, or just because it happens to be the

110

bride or groom's favourite piece) still allows for a great scope of music truly reflective of the personal tastes and backgrounds of the couple involved. Thoughtful and sensitive planning with the participants can produce a service that is thoroughly satisfying. Of great merit is the marriage ceremony which is set in the context of the church's ongoing worship life, (e.g. a Sunday service) because it represents reality. Christian marriages do not happen in a vacuum, but within a community setting. When the rites are performed in the sight of 'God and this company' and 'this company' truly represents the caring community with whom the couple is sure to be involved as they get established and begin their married life, then a strong bond is created. When the celebrant addresses the congregation with the question, 'Will you who have witnessed these promises do all in your power to uphold these two persons in their marriage?' and the people respond with conviction, 'WE WILL,' the powers of darkness tremble. We who plan liturgies are helpless to create this resounding affirmation to the wedded couple. It is a work of the Spirit of God in the assembled community of faith. We can only reflect what is true for those assembled in the last analysis, and point with hope to a resurrected Lord and a kingdom coming where sin in the form of divorce or its myriad precursors will be no more. But in our heart of hearts we can carry a vision of a community caring enough, involved enough, praying enough for one another, that the couple in question will have a fighting chance in our throw-away-marriage society. And we can ask God to establish that sort of worshipping community in the very place we live, with the very likes of us.

There is one gift which a choir can offer the worshipping family-of-God which is unique: the anthem. It should be just that – a gift; not a fixed happening, a never-to-be-varied occurrence within the worship service, but a gift of song to the assembled community of faith. When the choir *always* sings an anthem at the same point in the service, the results can be deadly. Too little rehearsal time may create an 'anything goes' attitude about their offering. ('Well . . . I wonder if they're sight reading *this* one?') Or, if they (the choir) have the feeling that a particular spot is 'theirs' in the service *no matter what*, the hearers are likely to detect, in place of the sweet smelling savour of a free will offering, the scent of assertive ownership. Not a helpful dynamic in building worship together! The choir's function can be kept alive, part of a living process in the week by week planning of services; then their offering will be genuine and not habitual!

Anthems come in many shapes and sizes. Some, because they are short and invite us to praise, make good invitatory (call to worship) anthems. Others, thematically oriented to the day's teaching and scripture readings, may be useful for times of response-through-reflection in the service. Still others express moods of praise, penitence, petition, thanksgiving, etc. and must be carefully placed within the context of the whole service in order to find their true mark in the hearts of the worshippers.

Anthems also come in a variety of musical styles, and we would do well not to get stuck singing only one type. Just as the choir addicted to four-part singing needs stretching in the direction of unison and antiphonal singing, so the choir of meagre abilities can be graduated into more confident part-singing by wise repertoire choices. In addition to published anthems we will find selections in many contemporary songbooks which are incipient folk anthems. Many rounds provide excellent part-singing experience for elementary choirs; they offer a minimum of notes to learn – since all sing the same melody – but a maximum of independence (i.e. learning to hold your own while other voices sing a different part.) The selection of rounds in *Cry Hosanna* songbook is a recommended resource for choir directors.

One 'hidden anthem' may be found in *Fresh Sounds* songbook, No. 44, where a method for singing Jimmy Owens' popular setting of the Doxology is outlined as follows:

First time:	<u>Sopranos begin</u>	
		<u>Add altos at mid-point</u>
Second time:	<u>Tenors join</u>	
		<u>Basses too (at mid-point)</u>
Third time:	All sing	

In building a repertoire for the small choir, two and three-part anthems should not be overlooked. The latter is especially useful when men are in short supply! Far better to have a confident baritone section than struggling basses and tenors. Three-part texture, while not as rich as four-part, has a greater clarity of sound. The vigilant director can detect, in the refrain of Tom Colvin's 'Neighbours' (see over) a three-part vocal arrangement 'hidden' in the right-hand piano part. (The key may be lowered a whole step to accommodate men's voices.)

Another attractive thing about this song is the opportunity to sing it with a minimum of keyboard accompaniment, employing instead the idiomatic (to Ghana) sound of small hand-drums. Nowadays it is possible to purchase interesting drum-boxes which are easily playable by anyone with a good sense of rhythm.

The group which finds a way to sing comfortably without accompaniment will discover a priceless gem. *A cappella* singing takes all the crutches away and reveals the voices as they are. It calls forth the capacity to listen to one another's vocal sound and

Simply, gently

Refrain

'Chereponi'
Ghana folk song

Je - su,＿＿＿ Je - su,＿＿＿ fill us with your love, show us how to serve the neigh-bours we have from you.

to become sensitive to blend, in a way that singing with instrumental accompaniment can never do. The uninitiated would do well to look (once again) to certain rounds as a starting point for *a cappella* singing. Thomas Tallis' famous canon, sung at a steady, not-too-fast tempo, allows the singers to become familiar with the comfortable feeling of singing consonant intervals, and the uncomfortable feeling of singing dissonances! Have singers prolong the unison notes (marked 'U') in order to 'tune' the two parts. Next time through, prolong the dissonant interval (marked 'D') to experience the discomfort.

Tastefully arranged, this humble hymn, found in almost any traditional hymnal, makes a beautiful, reflective hymn-anthem. One could use two solo instruments, e.g. flute and oboe, or two recorders, to state the canon as an introduction. Then stanzas could be sung variously by men, women, by men and women together in canon *a cappella*, concluding with a strong Doxology stanza involving all voices and instruments. May God grant us the gift of doing simple things well, and experiencing a true repose of spirit in so doing.

You will notice that we have left until the very last any mention of the anthem as a special gift to the worshipping family. This is because in so many quarters it appears to be first and foremost, the *sine qua non* of the church choir. Yet I believe that any choir who must sing an anthem for their own identity's sake is in fact a church-music guild, not a worship leadership group. In pre-industrialized society artisans' guilds served a very useful purpose indeed. They provided training and skills, and comradeship in the learning of them; they helped to diversify a society of limited scope and capacity for the dissemination of learning. By contrast, the needs of society today are for bringing about unity in our so great diversity, for drawing disparate elements into one, for counteracting the fragmentation with which our pluralistic society is riddled.

In this setting, a church which fosters a 'music guild' concept as the basis of choir membership aids and abets further fragmentation. For the discipline of learning music is a time consuming and demanding one. The chorister in a large church choir will have the necessary demands of weekly rehearsal time plus commitment to service attendance plus special events (regional choir festivals, training courses, seasonal happenings, etc.) These things, added to the necessary travel time to and from the church in a typical urban setting, will mean precious little time left over – for neighbourhood Bible-study groups, for helping a group paint the church hall, for car-pooling the youth group on an excursion, or serving on a committee to study the Christian education needs of the church family. Yet these (or similar involvements) are the very things which put one in touch with the congregation. Here is the crux of the matter and the real dilemma: how to provide, for the health and growth of our life together as God's family, a worship-leadership corps, a group of people truly in touch with and attuned to the heart-beat of that family, and thus able to provide for them sound worship leadership. Any choir which has done its musical homework, but failed in the equally demanding pastoral preparation, can be no more than a tinkling cymbal in the worshipping organism.

The dilemma seems to me a very real one. Many churches today opt for having *no* choir, rather than fostering the presence of a music guild in corporate worship. Others, influenced by highly-trained professional church-musicians, perpetuate the guild concept at the expense of folk worship. What is the path ahead? I, for one, do not think there are easy answers to the question, and will offer only one suggestion which may have promise. Perhaps within each worshipping congregation of people God will call out 'Levites'; people who have an extraordinary calling to serve God in leading the praises of his people; and therefore, people who will manage in a variety of ways (e.g. moving closer to the church geographically, lightening workloads so as to free up time for involvement) to give primary energies to both pastoral *and* musical preparations for worship. Without the former our music – and the people who make it – will be out of touch. Without the latter we may fall short of the Psalmist's exhortation to beautify our worship: 'God is king of all the earth; sing psalms with all your art' (Ps. 47:7 NEB).

9: Prelude to Praise . . . what is a good rehearsal?

> *A celebration is very different*
> *from a spectacle,*
> *Where actors or musicians play*
> *to entertain an audience.*
> *In a celebration, we are all*
> *actors and audience.*[1]

One night, after I had been director of a reasonably successful church choir for several years, I had a dream. In it, I saw the interior of our church at the close of a Sunday service. I could recognize certain faces in the thinning crowd. As the voices faded into the narthex two familiar figures appeared, both of them members of the choir and one a vestry person (in England he would have been a member of the Parochial Church Council). To my amazement, they both carried hugh push-brooms, of the sort which are used to clear large public buildings of litter. To my further amazement, that is precisely what they did: they set about sweeping.

From beneath the empty blonde-wooden pews came popcorn boxes, crackerjack containers and chewing gum wrappers! As the men swept, the aisles piled high with debris – leftover, obviously, from the service just attended. I was stunned.

When I awoke I was horrified, but I was equally sure that God was speaking to me through the dream. 'Beward of spectatorism in worship', God was saying. I have never forgotten the dream, or the message.

The Oxford Dictionary defines a choir as 'an organized band of singers in church, *usually* placed in a chancel' (italics mine.) The dream made me wonder whether the place we usually sat – the chancel – was part of the problem. So, for a time, we did an unusual thing; we sat in the back half of the nave during the Sunday service, lending support to congregational singing from that vantage point (a temporary and therapeutic exercise and one which may offer other choirs some food for thought.)

Taking into account the pastoral definition of choir which we have been evolving, what are the building blocks we shall need to bring it about? How can we build a pastorally-based choir? First, we shall need a particular quality of fellowship at the 'top' (which is really the bottom, for the leaders of the choir are its servants.) The fellowship could be described as trusting, supportive and non-competitive, a fellowship borne out of a primary identity as sons and daughters of God living in his kingdom. It is a fellowship based on life together in God's family, not the doing of a task together. The former has pastoral potential; the latter fosters a guild or club mentality. It is important, then, that leaders of the choir have some place for the outworking of their fellowship which is different from the place where they exercise their ministry, i.e. the choir. The choir – their assignment in ministry, as it were – cannot provide their principal place of fellowship.

The leadership of a choir needs to include a director, accompanist(s), other instrumentalists, perhaps a librarian, as well as pastoral leaders of the congregation. But suppose (some will say) the pastoral leaders can't sing! Hopefully, there are a few pastoral leaders (i.e. people with the whole congregation's welfare at heart) who *can* sing, and these are the ones who should be encouraged to join the choir. Their presence will be felt in all manner of helpful

119

ways. At times they may offer just the personal support the director needs to launch a new phase of the choir's ministry; at other times they may sense an undercurrent of resistance in the membership and find indirect ways (like conversation at the coffee break) to address it Because their concern is primarily pastoral, not musical, they can pick up all sorts of nuances which the musical director may miss. Trusting and supportive relationships build a trusting and supportive group; and the quality of leadership will determine what sort of choir we build.

When we speak of a choir as an 'organized band of singers' we are tempted to make 'singers' the primary emphasis in the definition. I would suggest that how we organize ourselves as a band is just as important as anyone's singing capabilities. Do the good singers group together like birds of a feather, leaving the weaker singers to fend for themselves on the fringes? This is not a tenable approach, pastorally speaking. Nor do I think we can side-step the problem of strong and weak singers by limiting our membership to the former by some process of selectivity (auditions, etc.). Not if we are aiming to build a group truly representative of God's worshipping family. Special attention will need to be given to the needs of the vocally weak, whether the weakness manifests itself in their inability to read music, or in rhythm or pitch problems. Each section of the choir will need leaders, people with both musical skills and a mature spirituality which enables them to give themselves freely to the 'weaker' singers. Theirs will be a ministry of encouragement and instruction.

It is amazing how much a weak singer can improve in basic musical skills when placed beside a strong leader in a choir. The relationship needs to be understood as a helping one; for only then will the way be cleared for the 'strong' to help the 'weak'. The ways in which the help is given may vary almost as much as the people and voices themselves! Bending near so the dependant singer can hear the pitch (or be alerted to sing quietly and listen intently) is one technique; using a forefinger to point upwards or downwards is another way of indicating pitch deviations. But basic to all is the underlying communication, 'we're in this together, and by helping one another we'll all get there.'

The key to the success of this 'helping' approach within a choir is the quality of fellowship which the leaders have established. It will communicate, far more than words, that we are members one of another, and will put to flight any hint of a pecking order, or a group of 'smarties' and 'dummies'.

It has been my experience that very frequently the members who are weak vocally are strong in sensitivity. By way of example, I will cite Kerry, a loyal choir member who brought with him not only a wandering pitch sense, but a background of mental disorders which manifested themselves in bizarre behavior at times. Unable to hold down full-time employment, Kerry came to work on the maintenance crew at the church and live in a ministering household located in the next block. He loved to sing. He loved the times of gathering with God's people; they engaged his mind and imagination, and in the hours spent sweeping the long corridors of the parish hall, he would frequently be impressed by a particular hymn-tune and begin humming it as he worked. Sometimes he would find me in the choir-room and say simply, 'I just can't get this tune out of my head!' then proceed to hum it for me. Not once, but on numerous occasions, it was the missing link in a liturgy we were planning. The Holy Spirit seemed to delight in revealing to Kerry the things which eluded us in our liturgy meetings! I came to expect it, and to give God thanks.

Another valuable choir member was Gay, a young

teacher whose chief gift was a ministry of encouragement to the director. Her eager, responsive attitude, her smiling countenance were always a welcome sight. On warm nights she remembered to leave a scented tissue on the director's music stand (very handy for mopping the brow!) A very weak singer; a very valuable choir-member.

In the accepting environment which a pastoral group can provide, many weak singers will in time become strong singers. Others will remain dependant singers, but learn to make an acceptable contribution because of their teachableness and their eagerness to offer themselves – as in the cases of Kerry and Gay. Strong singers who lack this teachable attitude can be problematical. A good solo voice does not automatically produce a good choir member! It is the desire to listen, to blend, to become part of a corporate sound-happening, which brings success here. A choir provides a little laboratory for learning to give place to one another and to live in harmony. As such it can be a valuable pastoral tool.

Another necessary building block for a church choir is the commitment of its members. A 'come-easy, go-easy' approach to membership will avail little either in terms of pastoral accountability or growth in musical skills. Far better to pray for, to wait for a group – small though they may be – to whom God has revealed the primacy of praise, a group whose heart's desire is to make the worship of almighty God the very centre of their lives. For the primary commitment of which we are speaking is a commitment to *be* a worshipper. Once this is established, it is amazing how other things will fall into place! Things like punctuality, regular attendance at rehearsals and services, willingness to serve the group in little ways, a prayerful attitude during services. All of these and more are the fruit of our identity as a worshipping people, a fruit which the Holy

Spirit will cause us to bear as we live out our lives in the church, God's gathered family-at-worship.

'But . . . but . . . but. . .' I can hear some say, 'our choir isn't *like* that. We can't just drown them and start over!' True enough. But what we can do is pray and work for pastoral foundations to be set in place which will enable the transformation of 'choir' and every other structure which serves the church's needs for nurture and growth. When we intercede with God, beseeching him to raise up *right where we are* a people whose purpose is to honour him with praise, we can be confident that we are praying according to his will. John the Evangelist tells us that the Father seeks worshippers (John 4:24). God's basic quest is not for singers, or Sunday school teachers; no, not even for preachers. It is for worshippers. Until the Holy Spirit releases this river of praise in a person, commitment is a hollow word, signifying some sort of debt or duty, and with it an unavoidable curtailment of personal freedom. So another part of our intercessory work can be prayer for individuals, that they (those whom the Spirit quickens to our memory) be released into a new freedom of praise.

But we must not stop there. For the entire family-of-God can experience *together* the high praises of God. Can we envision it as we pray? Once a dear friend had such a dream concerning the church of which we both were members. In the dream she saw the church full to overflowing with men, women and children, all actively engaged in praising God. They had obviously been taken up out of themselves into a place past self-consciousness. They were able to sing unashamedly, and lift holy hands to the Lord. The place was filled with a joyful awareness of God's presence. When my friend recounted the dream, it reminded me of the account in II Chronicles, cited earlier: when the people were *as one* worshipping God, the glory of the Lord filled the place where they were gathered.

Yet the dream left me speechless, because it was in no way an accurate picture of the present state of affairs in our half-empty church – and we both knew it; what then? I believe the Holy Spirit delights in sending such dreams and visual aids into our prayer-life; like a picture-postcard from God, with the simple inscription, 'Here! Have a look at this. *This* is my desire for you.' An interesting postscript to this particular dream is that God did fill the church with a worshipping people within a few short years' time.

Viewing the director's job as primarily a spiritual ministry in no way relieves him or her of the training aspect of choir leadership. Corporate time is very valuable. So, for example, if a choir of thirty is gathered for rehearsal and they spend ten minutes trying to make an inadequate number of anthem copies go around (and deal with the fact that some of them have missing pages as well) I reckon that the director, the person responsible for the ordering of the rehearsal, has caused the group to waste ten minutes? No, they have wasted ten minutes times thirty members equals five hours of corporate time! More than half a workday! The director needs to value corporate time, make the most of it, and never waste it.

What is a good rehearsal? Perhaps we would do well to direct our thoughts to some of the ingredients which make for a positive use of our corporate time when we gather for a choir rehearsal. Prayer is a good place to start. I would tend to give it prime time, and to start things off with it rather than run the risk of forgetting to include it later. Even if it is not *the* very first thing we do together, it can be a part of the opening portion of the rehearsal. We come from many different places, dinner tables, motor-ways, jobs, and we need to be gathered together. This drawing together can be done in a variety of ways: by a song, by a greeting, by a prayer, by all of the above. The obvious advantage of having folk musicians present is that 'gathering songs' are their stock-in-trade, and they can welcome the choir with a few such simple, sing-along songs as it assembles. Remembering that the means is the message, the inclusion of others-than-director in the opening rites of the rehearsal casts the aura of fellowship over all. It tends to place the rehearsal in its proper pastoral setting: that is to say, 'This is a learning experience set within the context of our shared life in Christ.' If there are visitors present we may want to acknowledge and introduce them before the actual business of the rehearsal begins. If one of the members has had a new baby, we may give thanks together. We may pray for a member who is ill. Whatever the content of our opening minutes together, they will reinforce our fellowship with God and with one another.

A vocal warm-up is necessary if the best is to be expected of the singers' voices. The warm-up need not be technical, and often several birds may be killed with one stone. For example, a hymn tune which is to be learned for the Sunday service may be sung in unison, first of all on an open vowel ('ah') and afterwards with the words. Lying as it does in a moderate vocal range, the hymn tune will get people singing freely and without strain. It is important to warm up the human voice by degrees, beginning with the middle pitch range first:

mid-range

women's voices

men's voices

Song material which is already familiar to the choristers, and passages from hymns and anthems which they are learning can provide grist for the vocalizing mill. For example, Mimi Farra's song 'Alleluia! Saints of God Arise', available in a number of contemporary songbooks, provides a refrain which is an excellent exercise for the breathing muscles of the diaphragm, as well as verses which lend themselves to the formation of blended vowel sounds.

A merry 'hee ha'

Hee hee hee hee hee hee ha ha,

hee hee hee hee hee hee ha ha ha.

Hee hee hee hee hee hee ha ha,

hee hee hee hee hee hee ha ha ha ha.

Verse — may be sung on various vowels e.g. mo, moo, naw, zay.

mo mo mo mo mo mo mo ... (etc.)

Learning to sing musical leaps with good intonation is a constant challenge. To focus attention on this and to encourage flexibility, exercises like the following are helpful:

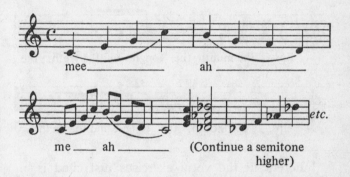

mee_____ ah _____

me ___ ah _____ (Continue a semitone higher)

Play the exercise with the singers and forecast the new key (a semitone higher) on the keyboard each time. Presuming that the group has been singing for a few minutes already, the outer ranges, both high and low, may now be exercised. For example, this vocalise could be taken up to G; 'Low voices now drop out', then on to A or B, before returning downwards, (collecting the low voices as you go!)

Good enunciation in singing requires the flexible and the uninhibited use of lips, mouth, tongue and teeth. The following exercise reminds us of that fact and helps us articulate. Repeat, a semi-tone higher each time, with increasing speed.

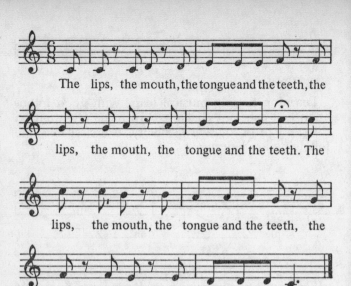

The lips, the mouth, the tongue and the teeth, the
lips, the mouth, the tongue and the teeth. The
lips, the mouth, the tongue and the teeth, the
lips, the mouth, the tongue and the teeth.

Inherent in the vocal exercises just cited is an element of instruction, usually the sole responsibility of the director in a rehearsal. Obviously, a certain amount of suggestion and correction will be necessary if the exercises are to serve their purpose. So also in the case of songs and hymns and anthems: there are certain technical points which simply must be put right, e.g. breathing places, accurate reading of notes and rhythms, etc.. The wise director will keep words to a minimum so as not to confuse, but also so as to keep the *modus operandi* one of a musical happening seasoned with words, rather than a lecture interspersed with music! The director must not get carried away with the sound of his or her own voice. In a music rehearsal, the song's the thing!

Equipped with two arms and an expressive face, the director has the means to communicate and instruct *as the music happens*. The quickest and easiest way for a choir to learn a vocal effect is to mirror what the director does. Smiling eyes engender good tone placement; exaggerated lip movements say, 'Enunciate!' Miming a 'Sh' and then placing a cupped hand behind one ear says, 'Sing quietly and listen to your neighbour so we can achieve a good blend.' So many messages can be mimed with no spoken words whatever! And the beauty of this approach is that the music carries on without constant interruptions for more instructions. A good rule of thumb for the director is, 'Never stop to say what you can mime on the way.'

Interpretation, another major ingredient in a rehearsal, depends for its success on how effectively we can engage the singers' imaginations. Painting a word-picture of the song we are about to sing will make a more appealing introduction than droning out the notes in a clinical fashion. One must see the forest before scrutinising the trees. Let's suppose you are about to introduce Calvin Hampton's 'The Church's one Foundation' to your choir for the first time (see musical illustration in Chapter 8.) You might say: 'Now here is a contemporary hymn of unusual and ethereal beauty. The melody seems to have no weight at all; it floats along so smoothly, like a spool of satin ribbon gently unwinding. Let's have the women sing it the first time through – on "noo, noo".' Such an introduction not only stimulates the imagination, but also gives the singer a handle on how to begin to learn the hymn.

Of course there will be times when repetition and drill are necessary. Be sure the choir understands why they are repeating a phrase five times; repetition is much more productive when everyone knows what the goal is. 'Now we're going to repeat that phrase on "bah, bah, bah", basses, so as to get the notes very accurate and clean.' Such drills can be fun when approached in a light-hearted way.

Hymns are perhaps the most neglected when it comes to interpretation. As we noted earlier, a 'hymn is a hymn is a hymn' and we may rip through them first in order to get to the really challenging stuff! The director who presents hymns in a cut-and-dried fashion has not immersed him/herself in them sufficiently to detect the different aromas of their tunes or the impact of their words. But suffice it to say that every piece of music is 'spirited', i.e. has a life-giving quality which is quite distinct and definable. We frequently refer to this as the mood of the song or hymn, meaning that which gives it life. The director should count it a part of rehearsal preparation to nail down these descriptions, to be able to put into words the life-force behind the music and words of the chosen hymns.

Perhaps, in giving oneself to study hymns and their meanings at some depth, one will discover hidden treasures of meaning which resonate with one's own faith-experience. Of such is the nature of testimony. It is an articulation of the word of God made manifest in our human circumstance. Somehow the link must be made that the truth experienced by generations of hymn-writers is the same truth we are experiencing in fresh ways today: no difference. Testimony, in the form of a short (two to five minutes at most) sharing of a revelation, an incident, something read, or heard, or seen, through which the Holy Spirit was able to speak, will make an important contribution to the overall content of a rehearsal. Nor does the testimony necessarily need to come from the director. It may spring from the fellowship the director shares with the accompanist, or the choir librarian, or one of the pastoral leaders in the choir. Whatever its source, it has the capacity to highlight, out of our own life experience, something the Holy Spirit is saying through the particular lessons and hymns we are using.

Exhortation is yet another helpful element in a

good rehearsal. It may come as just a friendly reminder about the tidying up of hymnals and folders after the service, or it may take the form of a mini-teaching encouraging the members to take more active leadership in the intercessory prayers on Sunday. Frequently the other pastoral leaders in a choir can provide a good sounding board for the director, and together they can sense what are the important correctives or 'encouragings' which the choir needs. If exhortation degenerates into a list of grievances, then it has truly degenerated, and we would be better off without it!

A wise selection of repertoire is the final element I would like to touch on. Something as old as 'Old Hundreth', something new, maybe Fred Kahn's 'Sing We of the Modern City', something borrowed from a culture quite unlike our own, something 'blue' enough to relate to the marketplace outside! We will need to tap into a great variety of musical styles if we are to serve the *whole* family-of-God in worship. And the musical director is the person whose skills of musicianship can help weave together this rich tapestry. It is not so much a matter of what music we use, as the way we use it, which is the telling factor.

'It's fine,' many will say, 'to use guitars and folk music in our services, but they just don't mix with the traditional hymns.' But they can! With a few rules-of-thumb to guide one's choices, music from different periods and styles can live together quite happily. First of all, we must analyze the elements of key, metre, tempo, mood, word content, and finally, musical style. Now compare two pieces of music in your choir's repertoire. How many common elements do they have? The answer will determine how successfully they can be used consecutively.

Considering the six elements just listed, how do these two examples compare?

Picardy 878787

French traditional carol

Unison

Let all mor-tal flesh keep___ si - lence,

and with fear and tremb-ling___ stand   *etc.*

EXAMPLE B

Anon.

Arr. Betty Pulkingham

May be sung as a 2, 3, or 4-part round.

Slowly, fervently

① Em   D   Em   Bm7

mp Je - sus,   Je - sus,

133

	EXAMPLE A	EXAMPLE B
KEY	D minor	E minor
Metre	Common time	Common time
Tempo	Moderate to slow	Slowly
Mood	Awesome	Quiet, fervent
Word Content	Veneration of the mystery of God incarnate	Personal devotion to Christ
Musical style period	19th century folk song (French)	20th century folk song (American)

The key is different, but the metre, tempo, and mood are the same or compatible. So also is the word content which emphasizes the adoration of the incarnate God. The musical style of both melodies, although separated by time or a hemisphere, has a folk quality, the minor tonality and simplicity of which make them compatible. They could work well in sequence (for example, during the communion of the people.) Let's suppose that the first, 'Picardy', is to be sung as a communion hymn with organ, the second a folk song led by guitars. To enhance the compatibility which these two tunes already have, why not transpose the first into the key of the second, E minor? The range is still practicable for a congregation, and the new key will permit an actual dovetailing of the two together. As the fist hymn concludes, while the organist is holding the final chord softly, the guitars can begin strumming the E minor chord as an introduction to the next song, i.e.,

134

Al - le - lu - ia, al - le - lu - ia, al - le - lu - ia, Lord most high.

(Guitar begins strum)

o = d

Je - sus, Je - sus, etc.

135

Nor does the organ need to disappear from the instrumental ensemble at this point. It can play a supporting role by supplying the bass line (16' bourdon and melody (solo stop).

The result of such a marriage of the organ and folk instruments is not just a musical mixing of the two: it speaks of a kind of give-and-take, understanding and fellowship between the organist and folk musician which is far more important in the end than what sort of music we are using in our service!

If four of the six elements already mentioned are compatible, there's a good chance that two songs can work well alongside each other, but as we have just noted, the relationship between the traditionally trained and folk musicians can be the hidden but all-important factor in bringing life to such a musical marriage.

The ingredients of a rehearsal may vary amongst the spectrum of elements set forth in this chapter, but the end result of a good rehearsal will be a sense of anticipation about the event(s) for which we have spent time in preparation. We will have worked hard, but with a sense of real purpose. And we shall have the confidence that, whatever our shortcomings as a group, we have offered our best and can confidently count on God to do the rest! When we approach a service with this simple trust God-wards, the end result will always be more than the sum of the parts. The Holy Spirit will honour our preparation, in order that Jesus may be magnified in his church. The event we call a 'service' will be a real happening, a unique gathering of the people of God to worship. We should not be surprised to find that the Lord sends us help from his sanctuary, that our mistakes are somehow 'covered', that in the context of a corporate offering of praise, our meagre efforts seem magnified and made acceptable in the beloved. We should not be surprised to find in the midst of our service to

God a new and deeper revelation of his love for his
people.

10: New Wineskins . . . the church—a crucible for creativity

. . . there can be little doubt that if Christianity is to address itself to the society of today, it must discover the place of folk religion, the cult and the social and community ritualistic experiences of that religion as a starting point for its mission and its evangelism.[1]

Referring to the great upsurge of cults in the latter part of the twentieth century, and to the way in which they have filled a vacuum left by the institutional church, Bishop Michael Marshall describes contemporary peoples as being 'starved of religion and the cult', and says that they have gone out to find the very food of which they have been starved, 'but now in synthetic and easily packaged forms.'[2]

What is it that the institutional church, with all her glorious heritage and wealth of tradition, is failing to offer people? Quite simply, it would seem, a place to belong and to know one is loved with the very love of God. A searching, following, embracing love; a love that tends to small details, a love that also liberates into growth and maturity. High tech has not provided it, the mega-church cannot provide it. Yet people are dying in loneliness the world over for want of it. Loneliness, according to Mother Teresa, is the worst disease which can be experienced by humankind.

In Scotland, there is a wonderful phenomenon known as the *ceilidh*. It is an offering of simple gifts; song, poetry, story-telling; within the context of a social gathering. It is assumed that everyone has something to share, in much the same way that St Paul assumed the same of the Corinthians gathered for worship. Both examples imply an accepting environment, where even timid souls can find the courage to offer their gifts. In such an atmosphere, generational and hierarchical barriers break down and a common humanity is experienced. A far cry from darkened rooms, each with its own illuminated box, where passivity reigns and conversation is almost non-existent.

Jean Vanier, speaking of the nature of true celebration in Christian community, says,

> *At the heart of celebration, there are the poor. If the least significant is excluded, it is no longer a celebration. We have to find dances and games in which the children, the old people, and the weak can join equally. A celebration must always be a festival of the poor.*[3]

How does this folk religion find a place of expression within the institutional forms of the church? The Holy Spirit will have particular answers – and very different ones – in our varying situations. But if we are prepared to ask the right questions, we shall surely find answers. We must not deceive ourselves into thinking that the institution is dispensable, for without it the new forms of expression will have little impact on the world outside, and no wherewithal to influence the future.

How can we encourage folk religion? Importing into our churches the 'sounds of renewal', a few guitar-songs to liven things up, simply will not do the trick! We must begin by asking the Holy Spirit how we can *create a sense of family* right where we are. Jesus himself said it can begin with two or three people (Matt. 18:20). In fact, authentic folk religion must begin in this way, for only deep, open, trusting

139

relationships beget deep, open, trusting relationships of the sort which characterize the kingdom of God. And where this foundational fellowship exists, a curious thing will happen. Total strangers will attend a meeting or service and say, 'It was the strangest thing . . . I felt as if I had come home.'

What are some practical ways in which we may be able to encourage this growth together as the family of God? I recall a time in a large parish when we decided that we needed to come together to worship as young families with small children. Many of us had had some previous experience of the sort of gathering where adults do something 'spiritual' while the kids are packed off to a back room; this was *not* what we had in mind. So we came together mid-week for a pot-luck supper around 5:30 p.m., then gathered in the church for a brief time of praise. Frequently, the minister drew from the children simple testimonies of God's faithfulness, ranging from answers to prayers for healing to showing a shiny new pair of shoes! Since the children did not separate the sacred and secular as adults are prone to do, their delight in little things could, with just a little help, be broadened into an expression of thanksgiving to God for his blessings. After this, one household presented a Bible story in action, a rough-hewn retelling of a story from our common history as God's people. Sometimes the stories were told in the form of songs, with the children acting the various characters' roles. Then we had a prayer of dismissal and went home. The entire gathering – supper, singing, teaching – happened within an hour and a half, making it possible for families to be home by 7:30 p.m..

Since the family of the ordained minister is frequently called upon to get new things off the ground, it happened that on the very afternoon of the first 'young families' gathering, our family was approached about presenting the evening's dramatized story – sure to be a pacesetter for what was to follow!

'There's not enough time!' I thought. But then, I remembered a little ballad I had written not long before – the story of Rebekah – and I managed to round up the children from their afternoon activities long enough to assign roles and do a quick runthrough. Living, as we did, in an extended household gave me access to friends and companions to aid the whole process. Without them, in fact, the whole thing might have been impossible. But we did arrive at the church on time, pot-luck supper in hand, and at the appropriate point shared our simple version of Rebekah's watering the camels belonging to Abraham's servant, and the remarkable consequences. The presentation was close enough to being completely unrehearsed that it had an appealing improvisational quality. We were clearly no dramatic giants, but we were enjoying ourselves and look – so was everyone else!

This hastily prepared piece of folk art was the catalyst for a whole series of such family sharings. Precisely because it was so unpretentious, people were able to look and say, 'Oh, well **we** could do **that**!' A slick, well rehearsed play might have remained a one-time-only event; this one gave birth to many offspring.

Holiday seasons can present special challenges in the life of the church family. Not everyone can afford to travel long distances to spend holidays with relatives, and some have no viable family network. Christmas can be a lonely time for single people, the widowed and divorced. During one such holiday season in an urban parish, a folk art evening was planned. Gifts of song and poetry, many of them relating to the Christmas theme, were offered in a very informal setting. Several people sang solos who had never done so before, and one very retiring girl offered a song she had written herself! There were family groupings also: a mother and two small girls sang a Christmas lullaby, another family gave a recitation. Afterwards there was time to chat over hot cider and Christmas cookies in the parish hall.

A wedding can provide the occasion for a genuine folk festival. Taking the family of God rather than the pages of 'True Romance' as our point of departure, the entire church can become involved. There are flowers to arrange, sandwiches and punch to be made, the baking of the wedding cake, even the design and sewing of the bridal gown and bridesmaids' dresses, and the provision of beautiful and appropriate music at the wedding (and the reception too). Indeed, there are no end of ways to enrich community life through the sharing of such a joyful occasion. But how often this event, intended to emanate from the community of faith, is privatized, sentimentalized and commercialized.

The baptism of a new member into Christ's body can likewise give rise to a community celebration. I had the privilege of visiting a small church in Australia on the Sunday when a baby was baptized in the midst of an ordinary service. Before the actual rite of baptism, the minister introduced the baby to the congregation; he carried her with great tenderness all the way down the centre aisle of the small church, saying to people as he went, 'this is Alicia.' There was a lilt in his voice and an unmistakable joy in his face. Bending low to make it possible for small children to see the baby, he would say, 'I want you to meet Alicia.' When he returned to the high altar and began to pray, Alicia still in his arms, one had the sense that the whole family of God in that place was presenting this baby to a loving heavenly Father, with great thanksgiving. As soon as the service ended, there was a party on the church lawn, with refreshments for all. This community had learned how to celebrate new life together.

It is interesting how out-of-doors settings figure into folk religion. In their book *Learning through Liturgy* Gwen Neville and John Westerhoff explore the phenomenon of outdoor religious celebrations in the Scottish and Southern American cultures. Outdoors is the place where we can have picnics. Outdoors there is room to dance, to play games. Outdoors we are put in touch with the wonder of nature; the birds add their songs to our praises. The eighteenth century Scots used to hold communion services on the grounds beside the church, literally within feet of their ancestral tombstones. There, in full awareness of the beauty of God's creation, and visibly reminded of the godly lives of their forebears, they would break bread together.

> *Slow the people round the table*
> *Outspread, white as mountain sleet*
> *Gather, the blue heavens above them,*
> *And their dead beneath their feet;*
> *There in perfect reconcilement*
> *Death and Life immortal meet.*
>
> *Noiseless round that fair white table*
> *'Mid their fathers' tombstones spread*
> *Hoary-headed elders moving,*
> *Bear the hallowed wine and bread,*
> *While devoutly still the people*
> *Low in prayer bow the head.*[*]

The Celtic preaching crosses scattered across Scotland remind us that at one period of history Christianity was a vigorous outdoors religion. Moving indoors has undoubtedly had many advantages, but it has also confined us to pews, filled our hands with lots of books, and in general domesticated our worship practices, as Westerhoff and Neville remind us. I would like to suggest that although we cannot turn the clocks back to the simpler days of a rural society, we in the church today need to bring more of the outdoors inside with us! Through simple songs and folk dance, perhaps we can begin to recapture the celebration of the whole of life in our worship.

The authenticity of simple folk music in the church was brought home by a recent survey conducted by the Episcopal Church's Standing Commission on Church Music (USA). Hymn words and tunes were listed separately by the number of positive votes for retention in the new *Hymnal 1982*.

> *Like the hymnody of other branches of Christianity, the hymnody of the Anglican Church is eclectic, being drawn from many different times and countries.*
>
> *The Anglican contribution to hymnody since the Reformation includes poems by Joseph Addison, Phineas Fletcher, William Cowper, Christopher Smart, George Herbert, Alfred Lord Tennyson, Charles Wesley . . . Charles Kingsley, Rudyard Kipling, John Masefield and Christina Rossetti; it includes tunes by Thomas Tallis, Orlando Gibbons, Thomas Campian, Jeremiah Clark, William Croft, Thomas Arne, Henry Purcell, Gustav Holst, Leo Sowerby and Ralph Vaughan Williams. These are poets whose works are found in The Oxford Book of English Verse* or composers whose works are performed in concerts. . .
>
> In the top ten texts, only one of the above poets was listed, Charles Wesley. . . In the top ten tunes, not one of the above composers is listed. The tune, *Sine Nomine*, ('For all the saints') by Vaughan Williams placed 33rd, narrowly beating *Three Kings of Orient* ('We three Kings of Orient are'). . . Who was involved in this survey?

Liturgical leaders, parish clergy and music directors of some 7,500 parishes.[5]

It is interesting that the only tune by a famous composer which came near the top was Mendelssohn's 'Hark, the Herald Angels Sing', a melody which the composer himself deemed unsuitable for sacred words! What sort of tunes do we find in the top ten? Half of them are folk song or simple chant.

Folksong has long been a popular element in hymnody. The implication is profound. Bela Bartok, who collected over 2,000 folk tunes, said: 'I am convinced that any one of our melodies that derive from the 'folk' in the strict sense of the word is an archetype of artistic perfection at its highest standard. I regard them as masterpieces in miniature, just as I regard a Bach fugue or a Mozart sonata.' If Bartok is right, the smallest parish can sing the best music in the world.[6]

The smallest parish can also fan the flames of creativity within its ranks, for there is likely to be at least one good hymn text or tune locked up inside each member! It is true that only the passage of time can authenticate folk music and distinguish it from the ephemeral or 'pop' art. It is also true that we can either help or hinder the process by the way we encourage or discourage the sharing of created song gifts in our local church. Our choice is sure to affect the folk music of the future.

We must not overlook the role of play.

The relation among dance and drama, religious ritual, worship, creative play, imaginative writing, painting and meditation is very deep in human life. Johan Huizinga, the great Dutch historian, has suggested in his book Homo Ludens that it may be a

145

real misnomer to call ourselves 'homo sapiens', and
that the term 'homo ludens', or man the player, seems
to be closer to the truth. It is the human's ability to
play creatively rather than think, that apparently sets
humankind apart from other species.[7]

There was a time when the arts were relied upon
to communicate the richness of Christian folklore;
you have only to visit a few famous cathedrals to
understand the role of the arts in mediaeval times.
Great paintings, frescos, stained glass windows,
pieces of sculpture . . . all add their colourful part to
the telling of the story. The mystery plays enacted as
chancel dramas or on street corners by travelling
bands of actors communicated the Judeo-Christian
folk heritage with immediacy and vivid detail. But
alas, the Reformation church in some quarters could
not contain the polarities of a sensory religion and a
naked individualized faith.

Perhaps the Reformers substituted one brand of
communication for another. By the time of Spurgeon
and Jonathan Edwards, the Sunday sermon had
become in Protestant circles the week's best entertainment, in the very broadest and best sense of the
word. The sermon was compelling. It had drama. It
had humour. It had a soul-searching quality,
providing a weekly catharsis from the dingy
humdrum of the workaday world. Today's preacher,
on the other hand, must compete with 'The Winds
of War' or 'Roots', not to mention the Winter
Olympics and the La Scala opera season, all brought
straight into the living rooms of the viewers. How
times have changed! And it would seem that the
church must compete, in some sense, with many
other appealing voices in the contemporary world.

Taking into account that fewer than half of the
people in the world are said to learn by abstract,
conceptual means, but rather by means of visual

images, we must look at the person in the pulpit holding the Bible and ask, 'How effective today is this form of communication?' Some preachers, to be sure, have a very highly developed gift of communication with words. But the point remains that unless they also have a gift of dramatization, the sermon may go unheard by half the congregation. There are many avenues the preacher may explore: the dialogue sermon, the illustrated sermon (using an overhead projector), a piece of folk art such as a short mime to set the stage for the sermon and stimulate thought, or a song to carry home the message and give the congregation time to reflect upon it. A preacher I know once asked a soloist in the choir to sing a particular song after his sermon on repentance and new life in Christ. The song was straight off the popular charts – Roberta Flack's 'I Tol' Jesus It'll Be All Right If He Change My Name.' The Black woman who sang it had a powerful gift of communication, different from Roberta Flack's, but equally as strong to carry a message into the listeners' hearts. The sermon reached many people at a deep level that day.

We remember ten per cent of what we hear, thirty per cent of what we see, and eighty per cent of what we do, according to today's educators. This being the case, we would do well to see and do a lot more in our churches. One of the universal favourites among Fisherfolk songs has been 'The Butterfly Song', which keeps one busy with hand actions while singing. Popular with the kiddies? Yes, but one of the places where it made the biggest immediate hit was on the Oxford University campus, where for days after the song had been sung in a meeting, university students were seen greeting one another with the sign of the butterfly! (For those who haven't tried it, it consists quite simply of crossing your arms with the palms of your hands facing you, interlocking thumbs, then allowing other fingers to wave back

147

and forth like a butterfly on the wing!) The 'homo sapiens' in each of the students was undoubtedly exercised by long hours of study and sitting through countless lectures. But the 'homo ludens' was bursting to get free. The playful child in each student came alive in response to this little song and its simple actions.

Of course, there is one place in the world where folk religion, with its freedom to incorporate physical movement and play, is quite alive and healthy. That is in the Third World. One example stands out in my memory. It was a Sunday service in St Paul's Anglican Church in Soweto, just outside Johannesburg in South Africa. A group of us, representing the Community of Celebration, were participating in the Sunday liturgy. We were warmly received by our Black brothers and sisters, a rather moving experience in itself in a country where white skin means oppression. At the time of the sharing of the Peace, an incredible thing happened. To the rhythmic strains of one of their 'own' songs (as contrasted with imported Western hymns) the people began to move out from the pews where they had been seated, mothers carrying babies on their arms or toddlers on their backs. There was a gentle flow to their movement, an effortless grace and beauty, as they converged in the aisles and made their way around the church, singing and greeting one another in the peace of Christ.

> *Amazing his love,*
> *Amazing his love,*
> *Amazing the love of Jesus.*

> *We walk with the Lord,*
> *We rest with the Lord,*
> *We sleep with the Lord,*
> *We wake up with him.*

*Through all of our days his love
stays the same.*[8]

They touched one another as they went. They
smiled. The movement and singing continued for
quite some time, and when it was over there was a
true sense of 'Shalom' in the place where we were
gathered. Never before or since have I experienced
such a grace-filled sharing of the peace of Christ. The
reality of Christ among us was palpably present; we,
who were strangers to this congregation, felt
completely included in the corporateness of the
moment.

Speaking of a faith that is adequate for the times
in which we live, Bishop Marshall says:

> *Such a faith must speak to the whole man and to all
> men and women in all cultures and at different times.
> It must be relevant and contemporary and yet it must
> speak of eternity and things supernatural. It must be
> flexible enough to be local and indigenous and yet it
> must avoid anything which is sectarian by affirming
> what is universal and international. It must be able to
> speak in many tongues and different tongues yet it
> must speak of the same truth free of discord and
> resonating with a rich harmony and counterpoint. In
> a word it must be catholic, or universal.*[9]

Liturgy is the church's shop window. For it is in
our gathered together activity as the people of God,
that our faith is made visible. Is the expression of
worship in your church relevant and contemporary,
while still speaking of eternity and things super-
natural? Is the expression of worship in your church
flexible enough to be local and indigenous? Does it
affirm the universal and international? Is it inclusive
enough, contagious enough, to involve people of
many different tongues, yet communicate the same

universal message to all? Are you able, together, as
the family of God, to sing God a simple song?

Notes

Chapter One

1. A. Carmichael (ed.), *Celtic Invocations*, (Vineyard Books, 1977), page 56.
2. St. Francis, 'Canticle of the Sun', from J. Blackburn, *A Book of Praises*, (Zondervan Publishing House, 1980), page 39.

Chapter Two

1. M. Kennedy, 'Isn't It Good', from the musical *Ah! There's the Celebration*, (Celebration 1976.)
2. C. S. Lewis, *Reflections on the Psalms*, (Geoffrey Bles, London, 1958), pages 94–95.
3. E. Fromm, *The Revolution of Hope*, (Harper & Row, 1968), page 1.
4. *The Book of Common Prayer*, (Church Hymnal Corporation, New York, 1979), page 302.

Chapter Three

1. J. Page Clark, 'The Tithe', from M. Barker, *Building Worship Together*, (Celebration 1981), page 44.
2. C. F. Alexander, 'There is a Green Hill Far Away', from *Hymns for Little Children*, (1948).
3. O. Nash, *The Face is Familiar*, (Garden City Publishing Company, Inc., 1941).
4. R. Bridges, *Collected Essays, Papers, etc.*, (Oxford University Press, 1935), page 71.
5. H. Jackson, 'A Monument in Bronze: Sacagawea', (Buffalo Bill Historical Center, Cody, Wyoming, 1980), page 14.

Chapter Four

1. J. Dallen, *Gathering for Eucharist: A Theology for Sunday Assembly*, (Pastoral Arts Associates of North America, 1982), page 38.

2. J. Poole, *Our Hearts Joy (A Christmas Meditation)*, (RSCM, 1982).
3. From the unpublished works of Roland Walls, and used with his kind permission.
4. Jones, Wainwright, Yarnold, (ed.), *The Study of Liturgy*, (SPCK, 1978), page 449.
5. T. S. Eliot, *Ash Wednesday*, (Faber & Faber, Ltd., London, 1930), page 18.

Chapter Five

1. E. Routley, *Music Leadership in the Church*, (Abingdon Press, Nashville, 1967), page 58.
2. B. Protzman, 'Travers happier in 2nd edition of PP& M', (Knight-Ridder Newspapers, 1983).
3. P. Gallico, *The Story of Silent Night*, (Heinemann, London, 1967), page 46 (italics mine).
4. E. Routley, op. cit., pages 90–91.

Chapter Seven

1. M. Morgan, 'The Evolution of a Profession', from 'The Diapason', October, 1981, page 3.
2. C. H. Phillips, A. Hutchings, *The Singing Church*, (Mowbrays, London & Oxford 1979), page 30.
3. *The Book of Common Prayer*, (Church Hymnal Corporation, New York, 1979), page 30.
4. P. Chappell, *Music and Worship in the Anglican Church*, (The Faith Press, 1968), page 18.
5. Ibid.
6. Ibid, page 29.
7. Ibid, page 38.
8. M. Bukofzer, *The New Oxford History of Music, Vol. III*, (Oxford University Press), page 107.
9. Morgan, loc. cit.

Chapter Eight

1. 'The Holly and the Ivy', traditional English carol.
2. Jones, Wainwright, Yarnold (ed.), *The Study of Liturgy*, (SPCK, 1978), page 29.
3. L. Dakers, 'Churches Without Music?', *Methodist Recorder*, 6 October 1983.

Chapter Nine

1. J. Vanier, *Community and Growth*, (Darton, Longmann and Todd, London, 1979), page 235.

Chapter Ten

1. M. E. Marshall, *The Anglican Church, Today and Tomorrow*, (Morehouse-Barlow, Wilton, 1984), page 139.
2. Ibid.
3. J. Vanier, *Community and Growth*, (Darton, Longmann and Todd, London, 1979), page 235.
4. Attributed to a man named 'Principal Shairp of Hawick', quoted in G. K. Neville and J. H. Westerhoff III, *Learning through Liturgy*, (The Seabury Press, New York, 1978), page 18.
5. W. J. Wolf, ed., *Anglican Spirituality*, (Morehouse-Barlow Co., Inc., New York, 1982), pages 126–127.
6. Ibid.
7. M. Kelsey, *The Other Side of Silence*, (Paulist Press, New York, 1976), page 187.
8. Marshall, loc. cit.
9. Transliteration of African folk song '*Uthando Lwakhe Luya Mangulisa.*'

THROUGH DAVID'S PSALMS

Derek Prince

Derek Prince, internationally known Bible teacher and scholar, draws on his understanding of the Hebrew language and culture, and a comprehensive knowledge of Scripture, to present 101 meditations from the Psalms.
Each of these practical and enriching meditations is based on a specific passage and concludes with a faith response. They can be used either for personal meditation or for family devotions. They are intended for all those who want their lives enriched or who seek comfort and encouragement from the Scriptures.

LOVING GOD

Charles Colson

Loving God is the very purpose of the believer's life, the vocation for which he is made. However loving God is not easy and most people have given little real thought to what the greatest commandment really means.
Many books have been written on the individual subjects of repentence, Bible study, prayer, outreach, evangelism, holiness and other elements of the Christian life. In **Loving God**, Charles Colson draws all these elements together to look at the entire process of growing up as a Christian.
Combining vivid illustrations with straightforward exposition he shows how to live out the Christian faith in our daily lives. **Loving God** provides a real challenge to deeper commitment and points the way towards greater maturity.

OUT OF THE MELTING POT

Bob Gordon

Faith does not operate in a vacuum, it operates in human lives. God wants your life to be a crucible of faith.
Bob Gordon draws together Biblical principles and personal experience to provide valuable insights into this key area. Particular reference is made to the lessons he leant recently as God provided £600,000 to buy Roffey Place Christian Training Centre.
Out of the Melting Pot is Bob Gordon's powerful testimony to the work of God today and a profound challenge to shallow views of faith.

BILLY GRAHAM

John Pollock

By any reckoning, Billy Graham is one of the major religious figures of the twentieth-century.
John Pollock tells the highlights of the Billy Graham story briefly and vividly for the general reader. Using existing material and brand new information the story is taken right up the eve of Mission England.
This is an authoritative biography which pays special attention to the recent developments in Dr. Graham's life and ministry. Fully endorsed by Billy Graham himself, the book is full of fascinating new insights into the man and his mission.

". . . fascinating reading"
London Bible College Review
". . . a difficult book to put down"
Church of England Newspaper

THE TORN VEIL

Sister Gulshan and Thelma Sangster

Gulshan Fatima was brought up in a Muslim Sayed family according to the orthodox Islamic code of the Shias.

Suffering from a crippling paralysis she travelled to England in search of medical help. Although unsuccessful in medical terms, this trip marked the beginning of a spiritual awakening that led ultimately to her conversion to Christianity.

Gulshan and her father also travelled to Mecca in the hope that God would heal her, but that trip too was of no avail. However, Gulshan was not detered. She relentlessly pursued God and He faithfully answered her prayers. Her conversion, when it came, was dramatic and brought with a miraculous healing.

The Torn Veil is Sister Gulshan's thrilling testimony to the power of God which can break through every barrier.

NOW I CALL HIM BROTHER

Alec Smith

Alec Smith, son of Ian Smith the rebel Prime Minister of Rhodesia whose Unilateral Declaration of Independence plunged his country into twelve years of bloody racial war, has written his own story of those years.

The story of his life takes him from early years of rebellion against his role as 'Ian Smith's son' through his youth as a drop-out, hippy and drug peddler into the Rhodesian forces.

A dramatic Christian conversion experience at the height of the civil war transformed his life and led to the passionate conviction to see reconciliation and peace in a deeply divided country.

What follows is a thrilling account of how God can take a dedicated life and help to change the course of history.

HOW TO MANAGE PRESSURE
Before Pressure Manages You

Tim LaHaye

Pressure is unavoidable. Everyone faces pressure in some area of their life. Even as you read this, you may be aware of pressures in your life that cause worry and tension and hinder your sense of well being.

The good news of this book is that there is a way to handle pressure so that it can become a creative rather than destructive force.

Tim LaHaye offers insights that will enable you to relieve stress and to live a more satisfying life amidst those everyday pressures.

LOVE LIFE FOR EVERY MARRIED COUPLE

Dr E. Wheat

Dr Wheat, a physician and therapist, has helped thousands of troubled couples improve their love lives and build happier marriages with his unique counselling methods. In **Love Life for Every Married Couple**, Dr Wheat explores marital conflict in a straightforward manner, focusing on the reasons why couples experience frustration and unhappiness in their love lives.

"Dr Wheat has revealed, again, his unique talent for identifying the critical issues in family living, and then offering wise counsel and loving support to those who hurt . . . I recommend Love Life to those who want a better marriage."
                                                    Dr James Dobson

RELEASE
The Miracle of the Siberian Seven

Timothy Chmykhalov with Danny Smith

The plight of the 'Siberian Seven' attracted widespread publicity and support.

Timothy Chmykhalov, youngest member of the seven, vividly recounts the events leading to the entry into the US Embassy in 1978, the long years of hoping and waiting, the uncertainty which faced them when they left in 1983 and finally the freedom which they found in America.

Release is a powerful testimony of faith and courage amidst intense pressure and threat of persecution. A story of hope and determination in the face of much discouragement.

SURVIVOR

Tania Kauppila

Born into poverty, forced to endure filth and slave labour in a Nazi concentration camp, how did Tania Kauppila survive? When Nazi occupation forces arbitrarily decreed that one member from each family in the Russian city of Rovno must "serve the war effort" for a "three month" period in Germany, 12 year old Tania insisted that she be the one to go from her family. She was young and strong and her father was needed by her sick mother and younger brother.

At age 12, Tania had already experienced incredible hardships and had seen more of life's harsh realities than most women ever see. When she left her family – the only security she knew – she faced frightening, unanswerable questions. How would she survive? Would she ever see her family again? Would she ever find the God of her father? Would she ever find peace?

Survivor is the story of an incredible life spanning three continents and five decades. It is a witness to the sustaining strength and love of a God who will not let go.

If you wish to receive *regular information* about *new books*, please send your name and address to:

London Bible Warehouse
PO Box 123
Basingstoke
Hants RG23 7NL

Name...

Address ....

....

....

....

I am especially interested in:
☐ Biographies
☐ Fiction
☐ Christian living
☐ Issue related books
☐ Academic books
☐ Bible study aids
☐ Children's books
☐ Music
☐ Other subjects

P.S. If you have ideas for new Christian Books or other products, please write to us too!